THE PERIOD SHIP KIT BUILDER'S MANUAL

THE PERIOD SHIP KIT
BUILDER'S MANUAL

Keith Julier

NAVAL INSTITUTE PRESS
Annapolis, Maryland

First Published in Great Britain in 2003 by
Special Interest Model Books Ltd.
P.O. Box 327
Poole
Dorset
BH15 2RG

Published and distributed in the United States of America and Canada by
Naval Institute Press, 291 Wood Road, Annapolis, Maryland 21402-5034

Library of Congress Control Number: 2003112203

ISBN 1 59114 662 3

Contents

List of Colour Plates

Between pages 80 and 81

Introduction

Some years ago an elderly man took his ten-year-old grandson to a major model exhibition. A large model of the *Royal Caroline* particularly caught the young lad's attention and, having looked at it for some considerable time, asked his Granddad if he would make him one. Granddad had never built a model boat in his life, did not know port from starboard, had never worked to a drawing, but, had worked in fine woods as a professional antique furniture restorer. Instead of offering the boy one of his favourite sweets while he more closely assessed the situation, he agreed, perhaps a little too quickly, to fulfil his grandson's dreams. Sensibly, he sought advice and soon found that the model had been built from a kit and that there was documented research available. Those people he consulted recommended that he start with something less sophisticated than the *Royal Caroline,* but it was too late, he had made a promise to his grandson. Two years later and after working several hours every day, he came to start the rigging and realised he needed some more help. For someone not used to working with drawings, it took a while to explain the ins and outs of rigging and belaying diagrams.

I was invited to view the model and comment on the results of what, by now, was nearly three years of dedicated labour. I have to admit to a little apprehension as to what I was going to find. Knowing as I did the story behind the building of the model, I dreaded the prospect of having to criticise adversely on what was intended to be the grandson's pride and joy. As it turned out, my fears were totally unfounded and, in fact, what I found was one of the nicest kit-built models I had ever seen. The man has now been bitten by the boat-building bug and is currently considering making another equally complex model, with the help of his now, thirteen-year-old grandson.

This story just goes to highlight what model boat building is all about, enjoyment, creativity, the demonstration of craftsmanship and a lot of learning thrown in for good measure. Where can you buy pride of achievement? Certainly, the look in the grandson's eyes must have been worth every painstaking hour spent building the model.

I would also use the story to support my standpoint that models built from kits are not necessarily inferior to those that are scratch-built and, in fact, provide the very best means by which the inexperienced can be introduced to the hobby.

Having said that, it is necessary to realise that there are some limitations about even the best of kits. The first point to remember is that they are keenly priced, commercial products and have to sell in quantity in order that the manufacturer can recoup his investment. Therefore, one does not find an abundance of spare material or fittings in the kit although, these days, the quality of what is provided has been greatly improved. So, where do kits often fall down? Poor instruction manuals and inadequate research are the prime examples, both of these usually falling foul of translating problems from the manufacturer's mother tongue into the English language. The research aspect often involves a double whammy in that the original source of data was in English, translated into another language, then put back into English. Fortunately, there are now two major British producers in the market place who have recognised the previous shortcomings of kit production and who are now very successfully doing something about them. In fact, since about 1999 there has been a very marked improvement in quality both in terms of accuracy and design.

So, with all these so-called faults, why buy a kit in the first place? The easy answer is convenience. The provision of accurately pre-cut parts, photo-etched and cast decorative pieces and fittings, reduces the need for a sophisticated workshop and tool kit. It allows the average craftsman, or even beginner, to produce a model that might otherwise be beyond his facilities. The kit lays down a more or less mandatory building procedure that teaches the fundamentals of construction and rigging that can serve well for the entire career of the model maker. It does not try to reproduce traditional shipbuilding techniques, but I do not see that as relevant unless you wish to demonstrate that particular skill or discipline, in which case you are going to be looking at in-depth research and a project outside the scope of today's kits anyway.

This book is an attempt to attract the newcomer to model making into the realm of period ships and to encourage those already bitten with the bug to raise their aims and ambitions into what is a thoroughly engrossing hobby. I make absolutely no claim that the methods and techniques that are portrayed in this book are *the* best, simply that they have been used and refined over many years of model making and that they work. As such, I would suggest that they make a good starting point and, if necessary, can be adapted or discarded according to personal preferences. Everyone will develop his or her own preferred solutions to particular problems, which is all part of the enjoyment of the hobby. True model makers never claim that their methods are *the* best, only that they are *the best for them* and, if at the end of the day the finished model achieves its aims, there should be no further argument.

The photographs contained in the following chapters are not of one particular model but have been selected to specifically illustrate a relative point or comment in the text.

Acknowledgements

It would be remiss of me not to acknowledge the help and support that I have received, not only during the preparation of this book, but in some cases, over many years of model making and writing. John Cundell, the editor of *Model Boats* magazine, a helpful friend of many years standing, has always been a tower of strength; Andrew Horne of *Euro Models* and John Wright of *JoTiKa Ltd.*, I thank for their practical support, and Chris Watton of *Victory Models Ltd.*, a model maker of international repute, I thank for sharing his knowledge of all aspects of model ship building. Finally, there is no way that I could have completed this work without the backup and encouragement of my wife Edna who, although sadly can no longer assist in a practical manner, nevertheless continues to be there for me.

Keith Julier 2003

CHAPTER ONE

Choosing Your Kit

The list of vessels available in kit form gets increasingly longer year-by-year and ranges from relatively simple coastal vessels through to large-scale first-rate ships of the line. However, unlike Granddad in the Introduction, do take time to consider all the implications of the project ahead. Be honest about your own capabilities and craftsmanship, remembering that a kit is not purely an assembly job with all pre-made pieces that click together and made permanent with a touch of glue. Get to know enough about your intended project to know what you are letting yourself in for. I am not talking about in-depth research here, but an appreciation of the content of the task ahead. Some kits indicate on the box the level of experience required and, if not, the retailer will usually be more than happy to offer advice. Many of the kits available have been reviewed by *Model Boats* magazine and feature in the *Period Ship Handbook* series of publications. These provide an excellent insight into their contents, the standard of craftsmanship required, the tools needed and whether you are getting reasonable value for your money. Further information is also available on the Internet, many distributors and modelling retailers having their own websites. If your choice of subject is a well-known vessel, your local library may well have some useful information about the actual ship and its history or, there again, a browse on the Internet may prove useful.

It may seem unimportant at this stage, but it really does help to establish in your own mind your aims in building the model. Are you going to build a representative model that is more for decorative purposes in your office or study or one that also achieves historical accuracy? Do you want to rig your model with, or without, sails? It is always wise to have a target, but not be over ambitious. A finished job that fulfils your aims gives wonderful self-satisfaction - next time you can always aim a little higher. Besides which, the answers to all of these questions are all things that can influence the choice of kit.

Having satisfied yourself that you have made a viable choice of subject, you may now be faced with selecting that particular subject from amongst the products of several manufacturers. For example, I can immediately call to mind five kits for *H.M.S. Victory*, with probably more on the way as we approach the 200th Anniversary of Trafalgar. So where do you start, and how do you make your choice?

First of all consider scale and the size of the finished model. How much space do you have in which to build the model? There are no extra prizes for the model made entirely on the dining room table using only a razor blade and a piece of sandpaper.

In practical terms you really need a bench that is about twice the overall length of the finished model. Once the hull construction is fairly advanced, you will need somewhere *adjacent* to put it while you work on things like deck fittings; the cupboard under the stairs is not a first choice! A major consideration is manoeuvrability when rigging. You have constantly to change from working on the port to the starboard side and, if you don't have an "island" bench, the model either has to be picked up and turned, or you have to have enough room to swing it on some sort of turntable device. Size will also matter when considering where the model is to be displayed.

Scale undoubtedly has an effect on the amount of detail built into a model. This is a little more complex than you might at first think. In general terms, the larger the scale, the greater the amount of detail which, in turn, often demands a greater degree of craftsmanship. Too small a scale and you may finish up with a rather sparse looking ship and some clever person pointing out that you haven't got a ships' binnacle. On the other hand, one should not equate scale to difficulty in construction. In many instances the larger model is easier to make, there is just a lot more of it, requiring greater attention to detail. The bigger model provides more space for getting your hands and fingers around the rigging, particularly if you have chosen to rig sails.

Price will certainly be a factor controlling the choice of kit. If your bank balance will run to it then go for the best value for money. *This is not necessarily the most costly*.

Value means different things to different model makers. Some look for greater research and historical accuracy, whereas others might look at the fittings content or the degree of pre-cutting provided. Yet others are more concerned as to the provision of comprehensive instructions and drawings. This is why I said that it is important to set your target, know what *you* want, acknowledge *your* standard of craftsmanship, and choose accordingly. One thing is certain, the overall value and quality of kits has improved enormously over the last few years. The market place is very competitive and poor products don't last very long. There is no such thing as the perfect kit, but it also has to

be said that it is a number of years since I came across a real dud one. Today, they all have something to offer it's just that some offer more than others do!

Obviously, it is best to get to examine the kit before purchase so that you can be sure that it suits your requirements but, in this day and age, you don't find a model shop in every town and you may have to resort to mail order. Most sources have an enthusiastic staff who will listen to your needs and offer help accordingly but, bearing in mind your financial outlay, the added cost of travel to see the kit is well worth considering. The *Mailboat* pages of *Model Boats* magazine also provide a forum for seeking information and exchanging views. Alternatively, there is the Model Boats website at *www.modelboats.co.uk* where again there is the facility to correspond and seek help.

If you are fortunate enough to be able to look in the box before you part with your money, what should you look for? Do not get carried away by a mass of gleaming brassy fittings, in the end they don't make a poor model into a good one. Much will depend on your level of model making expertise and the sort of target you have set for yourself. The picture on the box is normally the first sight one has of the completed model and it can be an instant guide as to whether you are making a wise choice.

Most people will probably look at the drawings and instruction manual initially, not only to view the construction detail but also to see how well the rigging and belaying diagrams are laid out. A good instruction manual is an absolute must, particularly for the novice. It will usually tell you not only what to do, but *when* to do it.

It is always helpful to see a parts list included, either in the drawings or the manual. Numbered parts cross-referenced to the drawings, and properly identified, are encouraging signs that someone has given the production of the kit some constructive thought. A ready indication as to the material from which they are to be fabricated is also helpful.

Drawings usually reflect the sequence of building the model and the earlier sheets will

Fig. 1.1 A typical sheet of etched brass parts.

concentrate on the construction of the hull and deck fittings before moving on to the making of the masts and yards. Perspective or exploded views for the more complex parts of the model are a good sign. The later sheets will normally be dedicated to the rigging of the model and show the start point and path of the rigging down to deck level. A comprehensive belaying diagram is as essential to the more experienced model maker as it is to the beginner. This should show where the lower ends of the rigging have to be belayed and often indicates, by a sequence of numbering, the order in which the rigging should be put up.

The quality of the timber is usually fairly easy to assess and bundles of straight and fine-grained strips bode well. These checks should equally apply to dowel rods that are provided where any warps or twists are totally unacceptable. A point often overlooked, however, is consistency of colour. This can be particularly important if the model is to have a natural wood finish, a feature often preferred by period ship modellers. So, it is worth having a special look at the timbers provided for finished surfaces to ensure that they are all of the same basic shade.

Pre-cut parts in various thickness sheet materials are arguably the area in which the greatest improvement has been made to kits over the years. The process usually involves computer controlled laser cutting, being evident by the discoloured or burnt effect to the edges of the parts. computer numerically controlled (CNC) routing permits the use of a third axis of movement during the process, enabling varying depths of cut to be applied, permitting the provision, for example, of the joints pertinent to bitts and pin racks. Printed sheets outlining parts to be removed by fret sawing should now be largely things of the past.

A well-presented set of fittings will speak for itself. Look at any castings provided in the kit, particularly noting if there is any excessive flash where the pieces have come out of the mould. This can sometimes be difficult to remove. Even worse is offset, where the two halves of the mould have not come together correctly, a condition almost impossible to correct. Wooden parts for things like capstans, windlasses and barrels usually come from standard lists of accessories: these should be clean and crisply turned. Similarly, blocks and deadeyes should be well drilled and formed.

Many kits today include photo-etched brass parts. Some modellers like them and some don't. However, they are a fact of life and, if included in the kit of your choice, should be presented flat in a well-protected pack to avoid damage. A typical sheet of etched brass parts can be seen in **Fig.1.1**.

Rigging thread should ideally come in two colours, natural for the running rigging and black or dark brown for the standing rigging. If only natural or even worse, pure white thread is provided, you will be involved in a messy dyeing process. A good thread will be devoid of hairiness and be wound in coils or hanks. Thread wound around flat card can have kinks that are not easy to eliminate without serious washing and stretching under weights.

In some kits you will find material for making and rigging sails. This does not mean that you *have* to build the model so rigged. In fact, many would argue that sails do not look right on a full-hull model on a stand. More of that later; suffice to say that provided you remember that a model without sails has its yards rigged differently to one fully canvassed, it will be up to you as to how you finally present your model. What is pertinent is that the quality of the material provided in the kit can be a major factor in making that choice at a later stage. Thus if you spot frayed edges, you can probably forget sails. The colour or the material can also be a consideration but strangely, modellers seem to accept the dyeing of sail material more readily than they do colouring thread.

A feature that I always look for is a stand for the finished model. To buy a finished board and pedestals can add somewhat to the cost of the project. Fortunately, these days most kits contain something on which to stand the model, even if it is only a simple cradle, which with a bit of thought, can often be enhanced and made quite presentable. It is certainly better than leaning the model against a bowl of fruit on the sideboard!

When you are satisfied that the kit will give you what you want, it only remains to hand over your cash. Beware; don't forget that there are some further essential expenses to come, not least for adhesives and maybe paint and other consumable items.

Before concluding this section, I feel that a word about kit manufacture is relevant and that there are one or two points that the kit purchaser ought to bear in mind. First of all, do remember that the basic raw materials found in the kit are subject to manufacturing tolerances. The size of a dowel rod is never going to be "spot on" to its nominal diameter, and the thickness of a ply sheet will always vary according to its type and classification. Sure, there are materials that can be very accurately produced but the cost, in terms of kit production, can be prohibitive. The art of producing a kit is therefore a matter of recognising any limitations and designing parts accordingly. A typical example would be the slots in false keels and bulkheads, which, together, form the cross-halving joints in hull carcase assembly. The astute designer will provide slightly undersized pads in the pre-cut slots that can easily be filed to attain best fit. Some manufacturers produce their own faced ply and dowels, thus permitting greater control on quality to be exercised but, whoever it is that makes the required material, still has to recognise that the higher the accuracy and quality standard, the higher the cost. It is the balance between the requirements of the model-maker and cost of quality that sets the extra good kit apart from the rest. The cost of producing the "hard" stuff in the box is only one factor however, and the cost of research to get things right can also be quite formidable if taken to extremes. So, maybe before picking up the 'phone or writing the moaning letter about some 6mm diameter dowel than only measures 5.9mm, it might be better to consider what you are really complaining about and ask yourself whether you would pay more for your kit to get everything perfect.

CHAPTER TWO

The Consumables

Adhesives

As I mentioned in the previous chapter, in addition to the cost of the kit, there are other essential items to consider. Adhesives are an absolute necessity of course and, depending upon the complexity of your chosen kit, you will probably need more than one type. The chemical formulation of adhesives has advanced rapidly over the years and there are not too many materials that cannot be stuck to everything else. I normally keep four different types to hand and, while a particular project may not require the use of all four, I make sure that I have them on the shelf. They are shown in **Fig.2.1.**

The adhesive that will be used most will be general-purpose wood glue. White PVA is excellent for the purpose as it adequately grabs in less than 30 minutes and completely dries transparent in about 24 hours. However, one point to remember about PVA is that any excess should be immediately wiped clean with a damp cloth since, if it is later required to stain that area, the surface will have been sealed and the stain thus will not penetrate and leave an undesirable mark. Many kits contain etched brass parts and other metal castings, so cyanoacrylate and/or a two-part epoxy resin could well come in handy.

I would offer a word of caution concerning the use of cyanoacrylate (cyano) for fixing rigging. A mere touch of adhesive on the knot or lashing is all that is necessary. Some commercially available threads will, if saturated with cyano, become hard, brittle and liable to snap. If in doubt, use diluted PVA that serves the purpose just as well, but involves a longer wait before trimming ends. A further warning about the use of cyanoacrylate should be remembered; it gives off vapours that will affect the respiratory system and continued exposure in an unventilated environment can make you feel most unwell for several days. For any extended use of these noxious adhesives, the wearing of a suitable mask is advisable. An old glass ashtray is ideal for dispensing an initial drop of the adhesive onto before transferring it to the model proper with the aid of a toothpick. You *do not* apply the nozzle of the bottle directly to the model!

There are times when it is more appropriate to use a two-part epoxy adhesive. There are several on the market but in every case its success is largely dependant on adequate joint preparation, cleanliness and correct mixing of the two components.

Occasionally I find that the sticking of thin strips, often provided for deck planking are better laid down using a contact adhesive. I choose to use Dunlop's *Thixofix*, which, being a gel is easier and more convenient in application and doesn't string. Once again, the vapours given off can be a bit noxious, so adequate care should

Fig. 2.1 The four basic types of adhesive.

be taken not to inhale them and certainly keep the lid of the tin closed as much as possible during the sticking operation.

Abrasive Papers

Abrasive papers, or what most of us loosely refer to as sandpaper, come in various grades and types and will be used fairly regularly throughout the building process. Glass paper, garnet paper, aluminium oxide and silicon carbide are but a few and a selection of medium and fine grades will usually fit the bill. It is wise to keep spare sheets to hand because they don't last forever. As soon as you feel the "bite" depart, it is time to use a new sheet, remembering that a worn rough sheet *does not* equate to a fine grade. If you use a coarser grade of paper for rapid removal of material, take care not to go too close to the final level because it can leave some fairly deep marks. In some cases, you might not be able to remove these without going undersize on the piece in hand.

If your selected model involves a general paint job, then it could be that the use of fine grade wire wool will be beneficial, or even some of the very fine abrasive finishing papers.

Finishes

Paints and other finishes of one sort or another will almost certainly feature in your list of needs before the model is completed. Many model makers prefer to do minimal painting and rely on the contrasting shades of natural or stained timber to enhance to lines of their work. The Colron range of stains will satisfy most requirements and the use of matt or satin varnish to finish untreated or stained wooden surfaces is largely a matter of personal choice. Both adequately protect the wood and whereas some modellers like the low sheen of the satin finish, others prefer what is perhaps a more historically accurate, matt appearance.

If colour is an unavoidable feature of the model, the little tins of Humbrol oil based enamel will fulfil most modelling needs, most colours being available in gloss, matt or satin finish. Humbrol also supply acrylic paints in small pots and these too are well worth considering, particularly since brushes can be cleaned with water. However, this advantage may be offset by the fact that these water-based paints do tend to lift the grain and additional time may be needed for rubbing down.

While on the subject of colour, there is frequent discussion as to what is the right colour to use for various parts of the vessel; reds, dark blues and yellow ochre being particular cases in point. Before entering into any discussion as to whether the shades you have chosen are historically correct, it is well to remember one or two facts. Paints throughout the ages have always taken on different shades due to weathering. The techniques of making paint have evolved over the centuries and, as far as I am aware, there are no sample 18th century colour cards available! Visiting restored vessels in dry dock have colours that may or may not be a true reflection of the original. All of which leads me to believe that my choices of Humbrol 60 with a dash of 70 for the dark red areas, Humbrol 25 for blue and Humbrol 74 for yellow ochre, is about as good a representation as can be found. I would dearly like to be directed to learned sources that could definitively advise otherwise.

I mentioned earlier that many kits now contain etched brass parts. Most modellers recognise the fact that such parts need cleaning before the application of paint and wash the pieces with dilute washing up liquid. This may be satisfactory if you are going to paint directly with the required colour, but if you wish to guard against paint flaking or being chipped, this is not really adequate. For best results the parts should be cleaned with a solvent such as cellulose thinners, then coated with an etching primer before painting. For this process, washing up liquid should not be used as it chemically reacts with the primer. The other essential in this process is the wearing of a suitable mask or respirator.

Another medium that I like is shellac based sanding sealer. Whilst it obviously serves well for its intended purpose, it can also be used as a finish for the model left in natural wood. When rubbed down with really fine abrasive paper, it produces a truly flat and hard surface. This should not be confused with the cellulose based sanding sealer which, although ideal as a sealant, does not have the same finishing qualities as the shellac based product.

Fixings

Most kits today provide small brass pins for holding planks in place while glue is drying, but now and again you might pick up a box that doesn't, or you may just not be given enough, so it isn't a bad idea to keep a few extra to hand. Brass pins 10mm long with round, or domed heads are ideal. As always, quality is important, examine your purchases carefully and check that the points are sharp and not spade ended and that the heads are well formed. Yes, I know that you are probably going to extract them and throw them out after use, but trying to push just a few spade ended pins into pre-drilled holes soon plays havoc with your fingers. Pulling them out is much easier if the heads are well formed and don't pull off.

Le Hussard, 735mm long from the Artesania Latina kit.

CHAPTER THREE

Tools

Tools are more difficult to quantify. Obviously there is a sort of basic list of items, which are more or less essential, and then there are those which make life a heck of a lot easier, but not absolutely necessary given a bit of extra time and innovation.

A modelling knife (preferably with a range of differently shaped, replaceable blades), a razor saw, fine nosed pliers and side cutters together with a light hammer are, in my opinion, absolute essentials. A range of twist drills up to about 2mm diameter and a pin chuck with which to use them will cover the majority of drilling requirements. A small David plane will also be a useful tool to have. I avoid the type of small plane that takes a double-edged, razor blade, which I have found to be insufficiently robust and can flex during the cutting action. One of

Fig. 3.1 A basic tool kit

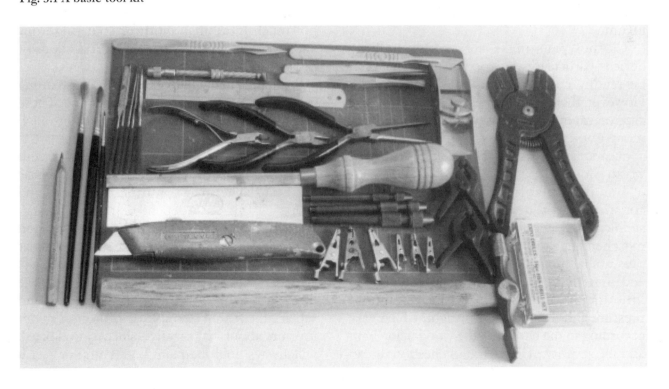

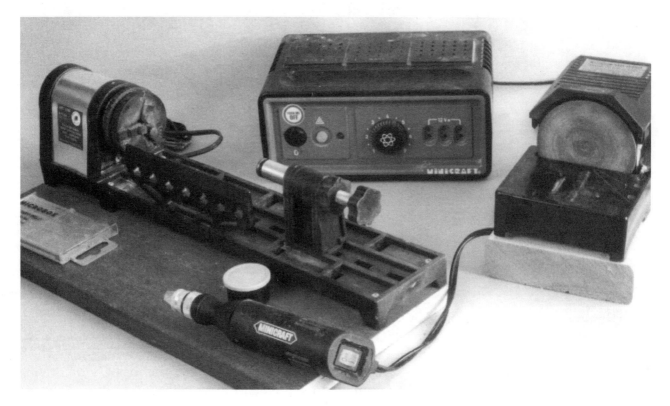

Fig. 3.2 Useful 12-volt electric tools.

my favourite tools, used specifically for rigging, is a pair of cuticle clippers. These are superb for trimming ends closely and provided that they are kept solely for that purpose, will last a lifetime.

Clothes pegs make very handy holding devices, particularly the wooden ones, which can be readily customised at the business end. However, there is an increasing range of spring clips of varying shapes and sizes available from most good craft tool suppliers. For small applications, electricians' crocodile clips are well worth a look.

Bending planks is a feature in the construction of nearly every model boat. A simple, yet very effective, tool that overcomes most bending problems is the plank nipper. This puts a shallow cut on the inside of the strip and, in so doing, induces the bend. It requires a little bit of practice to get the amount of pressure and the spacing just right, which vary according to the nature of the wood being bent and the severity of the bend in question. It can

often avoid soaking, but because of the way it works, it can only be used where the inside of the bend will be hidden from sight. Electric benders are available, but take care; some are not much more than glorified soldering irons and non too effective on the larger sections of timber.

For many years, I worked without a cutting mat, but now would not be without one. These self-healing pads come in several sizes although I find the A4 size completely adequate.

With regard to brushes, as is the case with cutting tools, the advice must be to purchase the best quality that you can afford. Size and shape will obviously depend on the job in hand. It is important that brushes be cleaned immediately after use with white spirit or similar brush cleaner. Good brushes, well treated, will last a lifetime. On the other hand, there are some modellers who will buy cheap brushes and replace them after a couple of projects. I'm not too sure about that practice, since a good brush will always hold the paint better, and deliver it

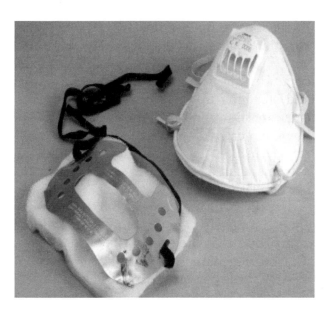

Fig. 3.4 Two simple but effective masks.

considered. I would suggest that an output of 50VA (Constant) with a peak of 100VA be considered minimum figures. Drills come in several designs, with various switch positions and the best choice is really the one that feels most comfortable to use. Some have chucks that require a key and others rely on finger tightening. For the small type of work that period ship models normally demand, the latter is generally more convenient.

The 12 Volt bench disc sander is a most useful addition to your powertool kit, permitting accurate mitres and square ends to be made. The 76mm diameter, replaceable Velcro mounted discs, come in different grades. The 12 Volt lathe unit is handy for tapering masts and spars but is only as effective as the quality of the transformer, hence the output figures recommended above. It doesn't help if every time you touch the work-piece, the overload trips out! This very basic lathe is also capable of making many small turned parts although this is not a prime requirement for the kit builder who should find everything needed in the kit. The electrical tools that get used most on my bench are shown in **Fig.3.2**

I will mention a small soldering iron, although when building kits their use is very

smoothly to the job in hand. A reasonable basic kit of tools is shown in **Fig.3.1**

A small 12 Volt electric drill is one of the first optional extras for any model makers' tool kit, but it is wise to buy a good high output transformer to go with it, especially if the later addition of further power tools, such as a bench mounted disc sander, or lathe is to be

Fig. 3.3 Perma-Grit abrasive tools.

seldom called for. That may change with the advent of the greater use of etched brass parts but, even then, I suspect that as far as period ships are concerned, there will be little in the way of assembly of one brass part to another to do.

A further sound investment would be abrasive tools such as those produced by Perma-Grit. Available in various grades and sections, they make for very quick and easy removal of excess material and are particularly useful for bow and stern block-work. Such tools are shown in **Fig. 3.3**.

While on the subject of abrasive cutting, it should be remembered that abrasive papers are more effective when used with a rubber or cork sanding block.

Finally, be wary of the "fast answer" gadgets, they invariably aren't. The old adage applies; if it looks too good to be true, it usually is!

Tool Condition

Tools need to be kept in tip-top condition if they, and you, are to produce the best results. Blunt tools are not only useless for working with, but are downright dangerous. An oilstone to keep them sharp at all times is therefore a worthwhile investment and should really be considered a part of the basic tool-kit.

If you use scalpels with replaceable blades do change them as soon as the edge goes off. The temptation to do one last cut has resulted in many an accident.

Similarly, worn glass paper is useless and should not be considered for relegation to the next grade down - it doesn't work.

Safety

Sanding can create a lot of dust, which should not be inhaled. So do wear a mask, even if only of the most simple variety. If you wear spectacles, then perhaps you should consider a mask with a built-in valve. This prevents exhaled breath leaking from the top edge of the mask and steaming up your glasses. Two types of mask are shown in **Fig.3.4**. However, if you are going to get involved with the more toxic substances like etching primers, cyano or cleaning solvents, then a specifically selected respirator is essential.

If you are fortunate enough to have a workshop completely independent from the house, a small domestic fire extinguisher is also a good idea, bearing in mind the flammability of wood dust. A small vacuum cleaner will help to keep the situation under control and is a worthwhile preventative measure. Of course, the ideal is proper dust and fume extraction, which will also take care of the effects of cyano, brush cleaners and other solvents.

Good lighting is a must. Two opposing sources of fluorescent light will keep sharp shadows away and thus help accuracy and not be a strain on the eyes. An additional, rather than an alternative, source might be an adjustable lamp for optimum working in some areas.

The matter of First Aid should also be considered. I guess that most of us have cut fingers at some time or another and have had to reach for the plasters, a supply of which I always keep in my workroom together with a bottle of TCP. However, I would make what many would describe as a typical model maker's comment. If you do cut yourself, try not to get blood on your treasured woodwork, it's the devil's own job to get rid of!

CHAPTER FOUR

Getting Your Act Together

The words in this section of the book are, in most respects, those that I have written before in other publications. I make no apology for repeating them because I feel that, particularly for the newcomer to the hobby, it is most vital advice. The first steps in the project are nothing to do with practical craftsmanship, so forget all about your tools and glues.

If the instruction manual or drawings contain a parts list, use it, because the identification of all the various parts in the kit will be useful and also provide an opportunity to check that everything is there. This is not often a problem, but should you need to request a missing part, or need a replacement for a damaged piece, now is the time to do it and correct identification is essential for a speedy resolution to sorting the problem out.

Do yourself a great favour and study the drawings and instructions thoroughly. Reading each step in the sequence recommended in the instructions and relating it to the relevant part of the drawings will pay considerable dividends as you proceed with the construction of the model. Build a mental model if you will. Probably the greatest significance of this is the fact that it will fix in your mind that some things must be done in a particular order. It is a sad fact that many of the more experienced modellers tend to ignore the instructions and go their own way, resulting in the later discovery that they have, for instance, some gun carriages that cannot then be assembled to a lower deck! So, the message is, do read the manual and do not try to be a "clever clogs." You can always reject advice if you think that you know of better way to do something, but do respect the time and effort that has gone into its compilation in order to be of help.

One very useful aspect of pre-studying the drawings is to identify where and when any painting can be done to advantage. Some fiddly bits certainly benefit from painting before assembly. I'm thinking particularly about items like head-rails which, if a different colour to the surrounding area, can be very difficult to paint after assembly, without the occasional splurge of paint going where it shouldn't; especially if age has robbed you of some steadiness of hand. Wales and rails are another feature that can benefit from pre-painting, in fact, any area where two features of different finish come together. It often helps to identify and isolate certain features within the overall construction and treat them as mini projects. Winches, capstans, deck cabins for example, all lend themselves to this and there is a psychological aspect to this way of working that often makes for better results.

If you wish to build your model to be as historically accurate as possible, then certainly you should do whatever research is pertinent before you start the construction. One of the more common criticisms levelled against kits is that they are often inaccurate. I have found that this is sometimes a little misleading and what is more frequently the case is that they leave something out rather than get something wrong. This is where you have to remind yourself that a kit is a commercial product and, the financial rather than the historical aspects largely decide what you get. However, there are one or two kits around that make nice decorative models rather than museum standard exhibits and, should you want the latter result, do your studies at this juncture to identify where you should deviate from the kit. In the majority of cases it

will be found that modifications can be made without having to buy additional material, merely using what is provided in a different way will often do the trick. Obviously, if this is not your first venture in model ship building, then the chances are that you will have accumulated a scrap box, which could prove invaluable.

Unfortunately, it is not easy to tell just how accurate the kit design is until you have the box on the bench and go into the detail of what is presented. A look at the picture on the box or the sales literature before purchase should have identified a total disaster, but that is a fairly rare occurrence.

So, which are the areas most likely to failure

Royal Caroline 1749

in the eyes of one wishing to attain a high standard of accuracy? A frequent failing lies in the fittings provided, anchors, capstans, pumps, windlasses, etc. There are at least two companies who have now taken this matter on board and, as far as is possible, provide dedicated parts in their kits. However, there are still many manufacturers who take these items from a standard stock list of fittings rather than design them specifically for the model in question. An inadequate selection of thread size and rigging block sizes can result in a top-heavy appearance to your model if these items are too large. All of these things contribute to what I call "The Near Enough Attitude," which of course goes back to what I was saying earlier about a balance between accuracy and cost. However, these are things that can normally be put to rights without much hardship if such detail is an essential part of your own personal brief. This is why I stated earlier the importance of establishing just what it is you want to achieve with your project.

As I have said, there is a gradual trend towards better historical accuracy, at least as far as hulls and fittings are concerned. However, there is much less archival information available about the rigging of specific ships and you have to largely rely on the specialist studies of others in order to reproduce what was generally the "Rigging of the Day" on your model, since there are few contemporary rigging drawings of the older vessels. Rigging diagrams in kits are usually based on such data and will normally feature all the major parts of the standing and running rigging. It is what they don't show that may make the difference between a reasonable standard model and one of exhibition quality.

If you wish to indulge in the more finite detail for your model, then the following works are recommended as sound sources of information:

The Masting and Rigging of English Ships of War 1625 - 1860 by James Lees.
Eighteenth Century Rigs and Rigging by Karl Heinz Marquard, this volume being concerned with ships from Europe, the Middle East and Asia and calls on major contemporary sources such as Steel, Chapman, Falconer, Rōding and Darcy Lever.
The Arming and Fitting of English Ships of War 1600 - 1815 by Brian Lavery
The Construction and Fitting of the Sailing Man of War 1650 - 1850 by Peter Goodwin.
Rigging Period Ship Models by Lennarth Petersson.

Should you chosen subject be among those featured in *Conway's Anatomy of The Ship* series, these too can be of invaluable help.

Books are expensive items to buy, but those listed above are still published and can often be sourced from public libraries. However, if the construction of period ship models is something on which you have got yourself hooked, then the expense of having your own copy for ready reference is well worth the outlay.

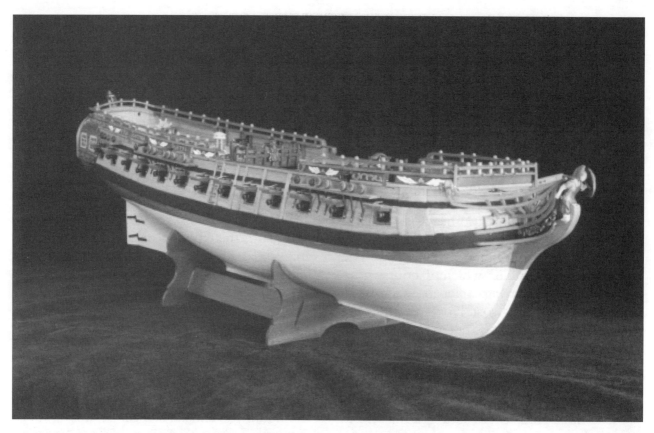

Above and below: *H.M.S. Ajax* 1140mm long from Euromodel Como kit.

CHAPTER FIVE

Building the Basic Carcase

Nearly all of today's kits subscribe to the same method of construction for the basic framework of the model, bulkheads slotted into a false keel. There is one notable exception to this process and that is the one developed and adopted by kit producers Billing Boats of Denmark, which involves building the hull in two halves then bringing those parts together to form the hull. Having built a couple of Billing kits, I found that while this procedure is

Fig. 5.1 The building board with false keel in place. Note the swivel clamps to permit clamping of different keel thickness.

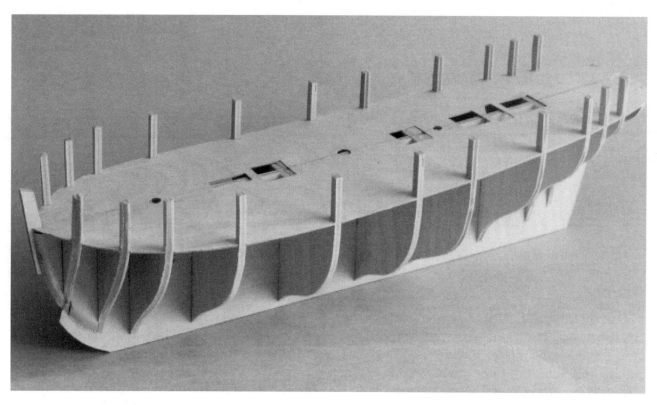

Fig. 5.2 The basic carcase with the false deck dry fitted to hold the bulkheads square whilst the glue sets.

somewhat different in its approach, it worked well and the claimed advantages of straightness were there for the taking. However, as far as I am aware, virtually all of the other major manufacturers use the whole bulkhead on false keel construction and it is this process on which I am specifically concentrating, although many of my comments will be applicable to both.

Straightness, squareness and rigidity are the keynote features to be attained in the initial part of the building process. In general, the bigger the model the bigger the problem, particularly when it comes to straightness, the main culprit being the false keel. Because of its length and the fact that it is slotted to take the bulkheads or frames, it is a prime candidate for bending. Even 6mm thick ply in this pre-cut form may be bent when taken from the box. However, this is not disastrous and the use of a building board to keep it straight until a later stage of construction is reached will usually do the trick, **Fig.5.1**. The other common cause of a bent false keel is due to stressing the part by trying to

Fig. 5.3

WRONG

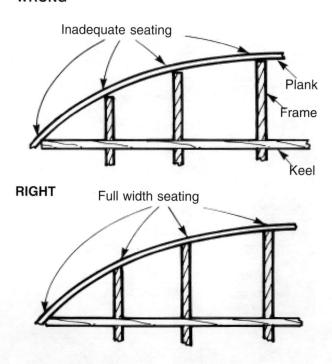

Inadequate seating

Plank

Frame

Keel

RIGHT Full width seating

26

assemble the bulkheads with slotted joints that are too tight. The resulting bends, twists and other distortions are, once induced, almost impossible to correct.

Before removing any pre-cut parts from their respective sheets, it is a wise move to clearly mark them with their part number. This is particularly important for the bulkhead parts, many of them being similar in shape and size. Having cleaned off any of the residual holding tabs, the bulkheads should be gently tried in the false keel for proper fit, the aim being a light finger-push fit, since there will be several occasions when these parts will need to be separated before bringing the glue into action. To attain this required fit, the width of slots in both bulkhead and keel will need adjusting. Having got that right, the next step is to get the bulkhead levels correct. On most bulkheads

used in this method of carcase construction, there is a horizontal surface or edge that will eventually support a deck. On larger models there might even be two, or even three, such surfaces and they will almost certainly be designed to coincide with a specific level on the false keel. The bottom of the slots may need some slight adjustment to get these levels right. The kit will have been designed such that the lines of the hull will be true when these levels have been attained.

Once the basic skeleton is in a satisfactory condition, **Fig.5.2**, the next task is to consider the edges of the bulkheads. These have to be chamfered to follow the lines of the hull in such a manner that the planks will be in total contact across the edges of each bulkhead, **Fig.5,3**. It is as well to consider doing as much of this chamfering before gluing the bulkheads in place

Fif. 5.4 Establishing the bearing line and thinning down the keel.

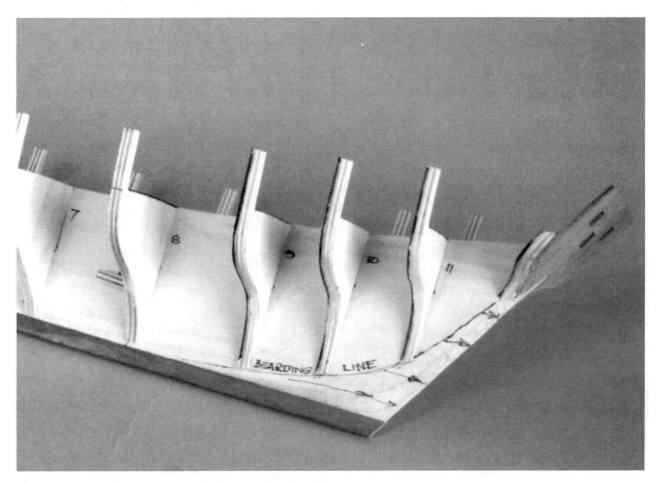

Fig. 5.5 Trapped nut in the false keel to secure the stand.

Fig. 5.6 Blocks to be shaped at the bows.

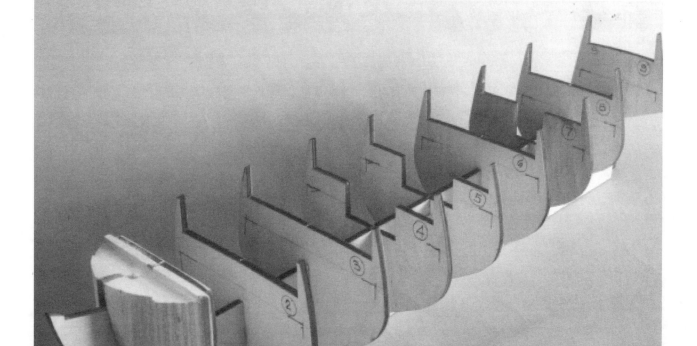

and it is frequently a good move to dry fit the false deck(s) in place, if possible, so that their curved outer outlines can be eyeballed and serve as a guide as to how much chamfering is necessary. The majority of the chamfering operation can be done by gripping each bulkhead in the vice and taking off as much surplus material as possible, using a combination of craft knife and file or, better still, Perma Grit abrasive tools. I am not saying that this operation cannot be done after gluing up the carcase assembly, but doing each bulkhead separately is easier and safer. To prevent breakout when performing this operation, always aim the file or abrasive tool towards the edge or face from which most material has to be removed.

Once the rough chamfering has been done, the next thing to consider is that area of the false keel adjacent to the sternpost or rudderpost. Not many kits feature a thinning down of the false keel so that the combined thickness of planking and keel is nominally the same, or thereabouts, as the thickness of the sternpost. Consequently, the model often finishes up with a step, or a total reduction of the planking thickness in order that these features all match and blend together properly, neither condition being very desirable.

An easy way to get round the problem is to first establish the bearding line. This is that line which follows the path through the bottom edges of the most rearward bulkheads. These positions are marked onto the port and starboard faces of the keel, the bulkheads are then removed and the marks joined up to produced the curved bearding line. The area from this line, to the edge against which the sternpost fits, is then gradually tapered towards that edge, in a horizontal direction, **Fig.5.4**. How much taper, I hear you ask? Measure the thickness of the sternpost and from it take the combined thickness of one layer of first and second planking; what you are left with is the thickness to which the false keel is to be reduced along its back edge. This results in both layers of planking needing to be reduced to half their thickness when rubbing down in order to finally match the thickness of the sternpost. This

provides a much more satisfactory solution, particularly if the model is to be left in natural wood. Obviously the matter is not quite so critical if the finished underside is to be painted or plated.

If the model is fairly large, you may wish to give consideration to ultimately fixing it to whatever display stand you choose to use. If this is the case, then your choice may involve the use of pedestals and the provision of, for instance, trapped nuts to be built into the bottom of the false keel, **Fig.5.5**. This is not an arrangement that one would normally expect to find mentioned in the kit instructions, but it is an issue that should be thought about at this stage of the build. There are two things to be considered here; the first and obvious one being, that the practical work to introduce whatever fixing device is chosen is far more easily done while the false keel is still in an individual state, with nothing assembled to it. The second, and far subtler one, concerns the manoeuvring of the model during the rigging process. It is far safer moving the model on a fixed stand than it is on a loose one that continually gets separated from the bottom of the model. It is also of greater convenience to those contemplating exhibiting their work in competition where, perhaps, more unfamiliar hands will be moving the model about.

The bulkheads may then be permanently glued in place on the false keel, ensuring that they all sit square to the centre line of the ship and are all seated satisfactorily to provide the correct deck levels. Fitting the false deck at this stage may prove useful in maintaining these alignments and will certainly add strength to the whole structure, again refer to **Fig.5.2**. The assembly should then be left overnight for the glue to properly cure, after which the final chamfering can be carried out using one of the planking strips to check that the chamfered edges are in correct alignment and that the strip sits down right across the edge of each bulkhead.

Before proceeding further, a second check using a piece of suitable dowel rod may be advantageous to make sure that the holes for

Fig. 5.7 Mounting blocks for false gun barrels. Paint the internal surfaces before planking.

the masts in the false deck do not need easing out to perhaps re-acquire the alignments established earlier.

The next stage usually involves any blocks at the bow, **Fig.5.6**, or the stern that provide a sound base on to which the ends of the planks are fixed. These might be provided, as solid pieces of timber or several layers of pre-cut ply, glued against the side of the keel and the faces of an adjacent bulkhead. Either way, the shaping of these pieces can be quite difficult and certainly sharp tools and clean files are the order of the day. There are devices on the market which are designed to hold awkwardly shaped

pieces, but generally speaking the final shaping is probably best done with the blocks glued *in situ* on to the carcase. PermaGrit abrasive tools are ideal for this stage of the work, but even so, considerable patience to get the lines and curves right is required. Again, the use of a planking strip helps enormously to get the shapes correct.

One point to take into consideration is the distance back from the prow outline of the false keel to the front outline of the blocks. When the planks ends are eventually bevelled and angled to sit tight against the face of the false keel, they present an increased thickness and, if this fact is forgotten, the layers of planks will come forward right to the edge of the false keel, leaving no visible stem post. In many kits, the faces of the false keel, particularly at the stem, are visible on the finished model as the actual stempost. It is therefore important not to damage these faces during the shaping process and a major contributor to such damage is blunt tools and careless filing.

Before planking commences, it may be necessary to introduce mounting blocks for false gun barrels, **Fig.5.7**. In some kits they come in the form of pre-formed pieces that actually joint into a false deck, in others the modeller may be required to cut the blocks from a suitably large sectioned strip of timber. Either way, their fixing to the internal structure of the model is absolutely critical since, should they come adrift when ultimately mounting the false barrels, they will almost certainly be lost within the hull and worse, the modeller has no way of replacing them.

A further series of blocks may be required to form housings for the masts. They may need drilling to accept the mast diameter or they may be assembled in a manner as to form a simple flat location each side. There are several variations, all of which have one thing in common – they need to be checked with a piece of dowel of the appropriate size, first to make sure that the dowel goes in the hole and, second, to ensure that it adopts the correct attitude. Failure to do this may cause all sorts of problems later on.

CHAPTER SIX

Hull Planking

The majority of kits have hulls that are double planked, the first layer being there to establish a sound base for the second. Therefore, the lay of the first planking is relatively unimportant and so, provided that there are no gaps and the planks have been well glued to the edges of the bulkheads, there is no reason to worry about getting the lay of the planks right. The exception to this is the planking above deck level, where the first planking may be ultimately visible as the inside of the bulwarks. However, this is not usually a problem, since there is little in the way of compound curves to contend with in this area and the planks are frequently parallel or have minimum tapering. However, such a cavalier approach cannot apply to a single planked hull, where everything should be more fastidiously tapered to conform to the general lines of the vessel as, indeed, does the second planking on the double planked hull.

Remember too, the point made about reducing that area of the false keel behind the bearding line. If you are going to adopt this principle then, although you may add any separate stem and the keel prior to planking, it is best not to put the sternpost in place. However, in some kits these features are added after planking anyway so this reminder would thus become redundant.

Sorting Your Timber

This is something that really applies only to the planking on a single planked hull or the second planking on a double-planked model. It is inevitable that the strips provided in a kit will vary to some degree in their shade of colour and, although I know of one manufacturing company that does make a serious attempt to batch incoming raw material, this can only minimise the situation rather than eliminate it. It is worth sorting through the strips to batch them into those that match in shade for the various areas to be planked on the model.

A further point to keep an eye on is their thickness. With modern manufacturing techniques and quality control, variations in thickness should not be apparent within a kit. However, manufacturing tolerances are a fact of life and, although batching for colour shade and thickness may be done, a rogue strip may evade quality control and really should be discarded, or kept aside for other uses.

Fixing

The fixing of the first planking layer is normally by pinning and gluing to each of the bulkheads, and gluing the edges of each plank to it's neighbour. Life can be made a lot easier by giving the pinning a bit of thought before hammering

Fig. 6.1 The Amati plank nipper.

away and embedding the heads of the pins into the planks. All pins should, of course, be started into drilled holes to avoid splitting the planks. However, if you choose a drill diameter that is a little smaller than that of the pin, then it will be unnecessary to drive the pin fully home. The tightness of the pin in the plank will be sufficient to hold everything in place while the glue dries and, for certain, it will be easier to pull the pins out before starting the subsequent rubbing down process. Don't forget to drill the holes parallel to the faces of the bulkheads and not square to the surface of the plank! White PVA adhesive is ideal for this stage of the construction.

Fixing for second planking is usually different inasmuch as you probably want to avoid pinholes all over the finished surface. Even when filled, they can spoil the appearance of the hull. Bearing in mind that this layer of planking often comprises narrower and thinner strip material, pinning need not come into the equation, it being adequate to use only a contact adhesive or, perhaps for the more experienced kit constructor, cyanoacrylate.

Bending

In my opinion, the bending of planks *as specifically applied to kit construction,* has

unnecessarily become something of a black art. The timbers usually selected for kit construction are not as difficult to bend as many of those woods chosen for scratch building and, it is not often that I have found it necessary to employ anything more sophisticated than a plank nipper, **Fig.6.1**. If the going gets a bit rough due to thicker or harder wood, then a good soaking before using the nipper will normally do the trick.

I do have a small electric plank bender, used for very small or tight bends, but I doubt that I have used it on more than three occasions in the last twenty years, and having built some fifty kits, **Fig.6.2**.

Before I start the planking process, I fill a vase with water and put a bundle of planking strips in to soak for a few hours so that about 15 - 20 centimetres at one end are well wetted. It also helps to recognise whether there is a need for more severe bending at both ends; in which case, I usually float a few strips in the bath so that the entire length gets a good soaking.

Application.

The kit instructions usually suggest a suitable starting place for the first plank. If such advice is not given, then deck level or the top of the bulwarks is a good place to consider, the former

Fig. 6.2 Electric bending kit.

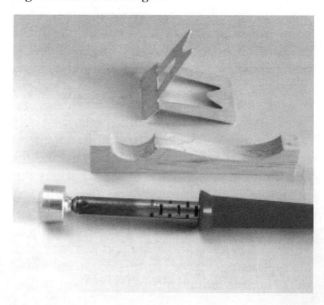

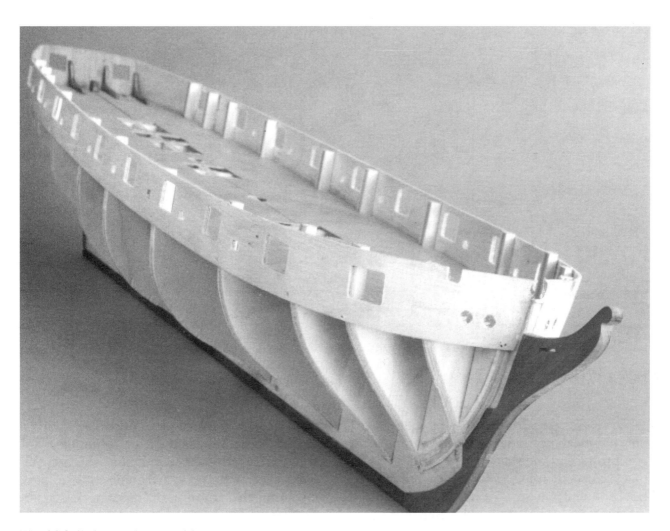

Fig. 6.3 Spiled ply bulwarks with pre-cut gun-ports.

being preferred. I normally start with an un-tapered plank, (letting it take up its natural curve) at the level selected, pinning and gluing a plank at the same position each side of the hull. This becomes your key plank as it were, and the remainder are put on above and below it.

If the design of the hull permits the planks to overhang the stern bulkhead and false keel, then it is usually easier to start plank fixing at the bows and work towards the stern, drilling and pinning the plank at each bulkhead as you proceed aft.

However, there has been a significant innovation in kit design during more recent times that involve the inclusion of "pre-cut gun-ports." I mention them at this time because this improvement in design comes in the form of

ready shaped, or spilled, ply pieces with the gun-port apertures pre-cut in their correct relative positions, which, being of the same thickness as the strips used for the first planking, eliminates much of the upper conventional planking work, **Fig.6.3**. Thus, the position of the first plank that does have to be applied is governed by the bottom edge of this ply part, more of which later in the section dealing with gun-ports. While on the subject of gun-ports, as planking proceeds, it is helpful to mark or recognise in some manner, the position of lower gun decks or the line of any false gun barrel mounting blocks. Such markings should be transferred from first to second planking so that when marking out the positions of gun-ports at a later stage, a suitable reference has been maintained.

Fig. 6.4 An example of practical first planking.

Tapering

Strictly speaking, tapering is something of a compromise in the shaping of a plank in order that it correctly follows the lines of the hull. To be absolutely precise, a geometric process often referred to as spiling should be used, but this is not something that can be reasonably expected to be within the brief of kit manufacture. The tapering of a plank of straight parallel width is, in many cases, not adequate to permit the plank to correctly follow the true lines of the hull. So, accepting that you are going to do a bit of cheating, the amount of tapering has to be determined for each plank. A little bit of measurement before you start cutting timber can pay a few dividends and perhaps give you

Fig. 6.5 Assessing plank tapers.

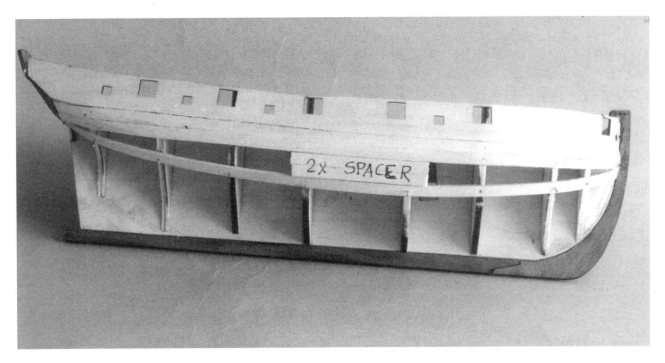

Fig. 6.06 The start of the "fill-in" method

an overall appreciation as to how the planking will proceed. I usually measure the length of the edge of the bulwark nearest the middle of the hull, and divide this figure by the width of the planking strips to be used. This gives you the number of planks that will be involved. If you now take a similar measurement at the first or second bulwark at the bows and divide this

length by the number of planks, you get a guide to the approximate width of the plank at the front end. The edges of the stern end bulkheads will frequently be seen to have a longer peripheral length and will therefore indicate that *stealers* will be required. Stealers are those shorter, triangular or wedge shaped pieces of planking, usually found adjacent to the sternpost. You

Fig. 6.7 Filling-in with two part planks.

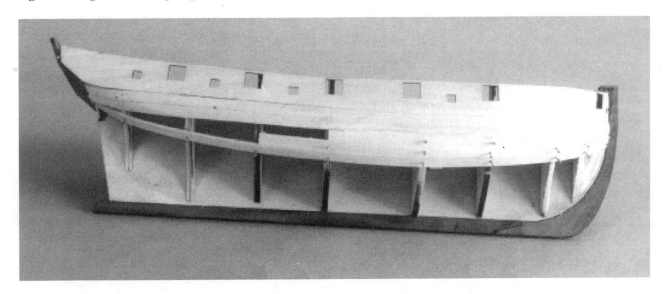

Fig. 6.8 Second planking leaving apertures to be trimmed at gun-port positions.

should now have a fairly general picture in your mind as to how the planking will probably look. However, it *is* only a general picture. You cannot assume that every plank will have, for instance, the same amount of taper at the front end. The entire tapering requirement is totally dependent on the compound curvature of the hull in question. Unfortunately, the pictorial representation of the planking shown on most kit drawings has to be considered suspect and frequently shows an idealised pattern that cannot be practically achieved. A more realistic result can be seen in **Fig.6.4**

So, having got your first plank, or pre-formed bulwarks on each side of the hull, you can now start planking in earnest. Take a strip of timber and, at a point about halfway along the hull; push it up tight to the underside of the first plank or ply bulwark. Holding it in that position with one hand, use the other to gently bend the forward end round towards its proposed position. Almost certainly, the top edge of your new plank will be found to gradually interfere with the lower edge of the first plank or ply bulwark. Mark the position of the start of this

interference with a pencil and also note the approximate width required at the end of the plank, **Fig.6.5**. These two factors will determine the length and degree of taper required for the second plank at its front end. A similar procedure is adopted if necessary for the back end.

Keep a close watch on the direction of grain of the strips being used, particularly if the thickness is below 1mm. Always try to arrange to cut tapers across the rising grain so that the cutting tool being used does not "pick up" and perhaps split the wood. Remember too, that several light cuts with the scalpel are more effective than one heavy push when cutting the tapers on planks. The shaped plank is offered up to check for acceptable fit, bent as required with a plank nipper, then glued and put in position. Holes are drilled at each bulkhead position working from stem to stern, putting in pins as the fixing moves along the hull.

If only the tapering of all planks was as straightforward as the first ones to be laid, life would be much easier but, unfortunately, as the planking proceeds towards the keel, the compounding of the hull's curves can work against you and further measures are required. The important thing to remember at all times is to ensure that every plank lies flat against the edges of the bulkheads without having to force an unnatural twist in the timber. Failure to do this can result in stresses being set up in the hull structure that could eventually distort the whole assembly. Thus, when it becomes apparent that the tapering determined by the process described in the paragraph above, indicates that the width of the plank at its extreme end is going to be less than, say, one third of its uncut width, a different procedure needs to be adopted.

I normally decide to use what I call the fill-in method. I move the offending plank down a precise multiple of plank widths until, when bent at the forward end, its top edge meets the underside of the plank above where it joins the stempost, **Fig.6.6** and lays flat against the bulkheads throughout its length. This leaves a gap in the planking to be filled in with sharp pointy bits at the front end. I take a length of planking and carefully shape the front end, pre-bend it with a plank nipper and then glue and pin it in place. This is not as difficult as it might sound since the tapered shape involved is almost a *sticky taper,* which helps the assembly process.

What can be difficult, however, is where the other end of the plank also comes to a pointy bit. Getting the shape right at both ends *and* getting the length of the inserted plank right as well can get a bit tricky. I usually solve the problem by making the plank in two pieces, with a butt joint midway across the thickness of a convenient bulkhead; a much simpler proposition, **Fig.6.7**. Shape the sharp end first then cut the butt joint to suit. Do not make adjacent butt joints on the same bulkhead, but stagger them.

Stealers

Strictly speaking, these short fill-in pieces should not have a sharp point at the end although, for first planking it doesn't really matter. However, when they are visible to the eye on the finished model, the thin end should be left at half plank width and the adjacent plank trimmed accordingly.

Chamfering

Where the ends of planks meet other features, such as the stempost, for best results the end surface of the plank should be compound chamfered across both the width and the thickness. Failure to do this will undoubtedly result in a weak joint and an unsightly one. Yes, I know all about fillers and that we all make the inevitable mistake now and again, but this is one area where it pays to at least try and get it right. Strictly speaking, one longitudinal edge on each plank should be chamfered along its entire length in order that there is proper edge-to-edge mating between adjacent planks. Unless the curvature of the hull is very severe, I normally anticipate that a reasonable amount of PVA adhesive applied when laying the plank will suffice, particularly for first planking.

Tools For The Job

In one respect, cutting wet wood makes life easier. I find that sharp scalpels, a steel rule and a cutting mat are the ideal tools for producing the tapers and chamfers. Where the taper runs out to the full width of the strip, I usually just take off the junction point with a David plane. If it is required to chamfer right along an edge, then the David plane is again the tool for the job. I suppose that, strictly speaking, the model-maker should be advised to hold the plank in a plank vice, but I normally hold the plank with one edge down on the bench with one hand, and plane the opposite edge with the other. This is not as risky as it sounds provided that you keep your plane well sharpened and honed so that it cuts smoothly and evenly.

Rubbing Down

The first task is to get rid of all the fixing pins. It is at this stage that you will appreciate that you didn't knock the heads down flush when putting the planks on. When you think you have got them all out, have another careful look to make sure; one pin overlooked can make a nasty rip in your finger during the smoothing operation. By the way, it is a false economy to keep extracted pins; they frequently do not drive straight when used for a second time. A medium

Fig. 6.9 Plated undersides simulated with wooden tiles on *H.M.S. Bellona.*

Fig. 6.10 Gore lines and copper plates on *H.M.S. Agamemnon.*

grade of abrasive paper should be all that is necessary to get off any high spots and ridges assuming that you have made a reasonable job of the planking.

Do remember to wear a face mask when rubbing down; both the long and short term effects of inhaling the fine dust particles are not to be sneezed at - pun intended. If you wear glasses, the use of a mask with an exhalation valve built into the front is worth considering; this avoids the lenses from misting up.

Having got the whole outside of the planking to its rough state, I use a palette knife or flexible piece of plastic sheet to go over the whole surface with filler. Modelite or even fine grade Polyfilla is adequate for the job, if the surface is merely a base for second planking. If the model is only single planked then, of course, a proper coloured filler to suit the finish required will have to be used.

When the filler has thoroughly hardened, finer grades of abrasive paper can then be used to take the surface down to required smoothness. Remember that if you are going to use a contact adhesive for second planking, then while the surface needs to be true, there is no advantage in making it dead smooth.

Wear the facemask again; this time you have to contend with powdered filler as well as wood and glue particles.

I would refer you back to the chapter on carcase building and, in particular, the thinning down of the false keel aft of the bearding line. When rubbing down the first planking, the thickness of the planking adjacent to the sternpost should be reduced by about half. After completing the second planking, the ends of the planks should be trimmed off and the sternpost glued into place. The rubbing down to approximately half the thickness of the second planking would then ensure a proper blend of post and finished planking.

Second Planking

Nearly everything that has been said so far about the first planking equally applies to the second. However, there are some additional considerations to be made; not the least of which, is the run of the planking. The fact that the planking strips for second planking are usually narrower, and sometimes thinner, than those used for the first layer, can be a great advantage in getting the line of planking looking shipyard fashion. Another thing to recognise is that the planking pattern that will normally be seen is above the waterline. It is in the area of the waterline and below, where the extreme compounding of the ship's curves comes into play and causes the modeller problems. The area below the waterline may well be painted white or even copper plated so is, therefore, not a worry in this regard. There is quite a large area almost immediately above the waterline that will later be covered by the main wale, which will also provide an opportunity to deviate from the planking pattern if necessary, since any out of line planking will ultimately be covered by the wale planking. These are all considerations that can be borne in mind in case of potential difficulties.

What cannot be hidden, however, are the ends of planks where they meet the stem of the hull. Every effort should be made to chamfer the width and thickness of the plank so as to make a good mating joint.

Planking at the upper level should be continued slightly above the top line of the bulwarks, so that this line can be ultimately established together, and simultaneously with, the inner, bulwark planking.

When applying the second planking, care should be taken not to completely cover the gunport openings but to leave access for tools to trim out the apertures later, **Fig.6.8**.

Hopefully, the standard of tapering will be such as to minimise gaps or other mishaps that might have occurred during the planking process, but should the use of filler be required, the colour should not be too contrasting with the wood or it will exaggerate the fault rather than disguise it. In many cases, it may be simpler to merely introduce a string of PVA into the gap with a toothpick, let it dry for a couple of minutes, then rub over with a medium grade of abrasive paper, although this is not a process that works very well at the above mentioned coming together of plank and stem.

A further tip at this stage is to see if it is possible to delay planking the inside of the bulwarks until after you have laid the deck, it can make this latter task that much easier.

The Undersides

The second planking below the waterline may be untreated, in which case the procedure for planking will be as that described for the area above the waterline. In many cases the undersides of the vessel will be painted with white stuff in which circumstance the planking can follow the same method as for the first planking, it only being necessary to provide a sound and smooth surface for painting.

Coppering

A more difficult situation arises when the bottom of the ship is coppered. This may be done using actual copper plates or, if you wish to simulate this condition as an enhancement to the kit design, wooden "copper" plates may be used, either way the application procedure is similar; decide where you want each plate, apply the adhesive and put the plate in place. For the wooden plates method, the conventional planking strips can be cut into short lengths, say 20mm for models at a scale of 1/64, then stuck on as separate pieces from waterline down to keel using PVA as the adhesive. Obviously the length will need to be adjusted according to the scale in hand. This provides a very fair simulation of a plated surface, **Fig.6.9**. The pattern for laying should be decided in the same manner as for the "proper" copper plates as the following notes suggest. Before getting into the intricacies of lining everything up, a few basics are in order.

The adhesive recommended is thick grade cyano with an almost immediate wipe over to remove any seepage from around the plate. This is important so that adjacent plates fit snugly against their neighbours. Equally essential, is to ensure that the plates lie tight down against the planking and, where the hull surface shows any sign of a curve, that same curve must be induced into the copper plate. This is not so difficult as

it sounds and a gentle squeeze, between thumb and forefinger, usually does the trick. Most kits that feature individual copper plates are for fairly large models that involve up to 2500 plates so there is plenty of opportunity to get the hang of it! Seriously, it really isn't difficult - just time consuming.

Inevitably, there are quite a few plates that need to be cut to shape, those at the end of each row and those adjacent to the waterline, for instance. Without doubt, the best way to cut them is to lay them on a hard, flat surface and use a craft knife. One of the self-healing cutting mats is ideal. Avoid the use of scissors; the shearing action tends to curl the copper and turn over the cut edges, thus preventing proper seating to the wooden surface below.

The laying pattern is largely dependant on the shape of the hull underside and needs to be given a bit of thought before embarking on the exciting job of sticking on a couple of thousand plates. The lines of plates do not follow the same pattern as the planks below and if you merely start at the keel and work your way up, there is a danger that the curves become too severe as the waterline is approached. While I was not able to find any definitive ruling on the establishment of coppering patterns, the information that did come to hand indicated the use of gore lines to prevent the patterns from becoming too complex.

What is a gore line? The most obvious gore line is the waterline itself, and it is readily seen that lines of plates curve upward, toward, and terminate at that straight line defined by the waterline. Some hull shapes require, perhaps, two or three gore lines. The way that I have found to easily decide a satisfactory position for the first, is to take a planking strip and lay it on the hull, such that it will take up its natural line when its top edge crosses the waterline at stem and stern posts. A line marked onto the hull at this position is the first gore line. The first row of copper plates can be laid along it, with subsequent rows added *above* until the waterline is reached. The second gore line can be established in a similar manner where the planking strip can again follow its natural curve on the lower hull and intersect the first gore line at stem and stern. The space between the gore lines can then be filled in starting at the top of the second gore line and working *upwards* to the bottom of the first gore line, **Fig.6.10**.

Use the planking strip as before until its natural curve reaches the keel. No further gore lines are required once this situation is reached and the plating continues in order to fill the gap between the keel and the underside of the last gore line.

I cannot tell you that this process is based on historical procedure, but it is one that model makers have used when scratch building, and one that has been personally adopted with total success. As for finishing the plates, you may like the shiny copper, or you may find it a bit on the bright side to suit your taste. That being the case, the shine can be taken down considerably by a coat of clear matt varnish.

One final word; the plating process is an extended task using cyanoacrylate and certainly long enough to make you feel really unwell if you don't take adequate precautions with ventilation or respirator. The vapours that are given off are not immediately apparent but creep up on you, so beware.

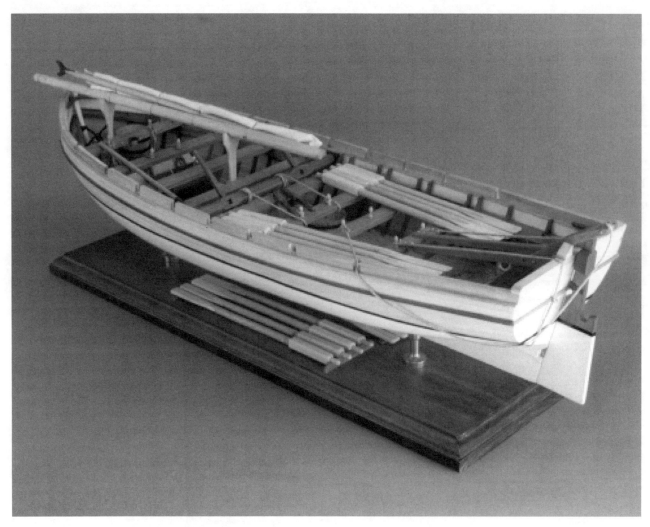

Launch from *H.M.S. Victory*, 620mm long from a Panart kit.

CHAPTER SEVEN

Deck Planking

Before laying planks, it may be necessary to remove any bulkhead extensions above the deck line that were there to facilitate the upper hull planking. In some cases, of course, they are used as supports for the inner bulwark planking and thus will remain in place. If they need to be removed, they can usually be twisted off with a pair of pliers but it is essential that any excess material at the break line be removed to be flush with the surface of the false deck.

Simulating the Caulking.

The laying of the deck on any model ship is the one aspect that immediately takes the eye of the casual viewer or the competition judge. They don't have to be specifically examining the deck, but any faults usually stand out and come to

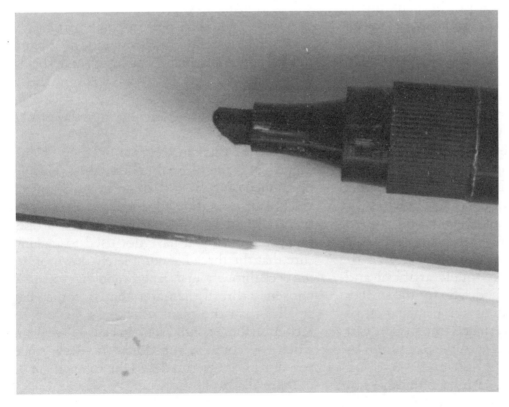

Fig. 7.1 Marking the edge of the deck planks.

Fig. 7.2 Butt system of deck planking

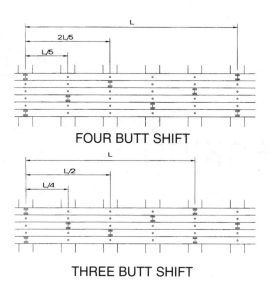

FOUR BUTT SHIFT

THREE BUTT SHIFT

immediate notice. Fortunately, the days are gone (I hope), where the modeller is expected to draw or score lines on a piece of ply to simulate the caulking between the planks. Kits today usually provide a ply, false deck onto which is mounted a layer of planking. How the caulking is simulated is largely left up to the model-maker and much will depend on scale and personal preference. This is not an area where it would right to try and recommend a particular approach, because there isn't just one that is correct for all circumstances. Every model maker of experience, will no doubt have his or her own favourite method, which will be first choice to try on any new model; but that same experience will soon indicate whether it is the one that looks right for the model in hand.

Scale is a major consideration and you do not want to finish up with caulking lines that would be seen to be grossly oversize or prominent. This looks totally artificial and completely spoils the model. So for the smaller scales, maybe just butting the planking strips edge to edge will suffice; indeed the shadow cast into the minute gap between the planks can be quite adequate.

If the planking strips are 1mm thickness or more, blackening one, or both edges of the strip with a chisel pointed black marker pen, before laying, can attain an effective simulation, **Fig.7.1**. The difference between doing one edge or both is very subtle, but it can be noticeable, and is worth trying on a test piece before committing to the model. The difference has much to do with the quality of the timber and its absorption of the ink but, in the end, the firmer and more robust line provided by blackening both edges of the strip comes back to personal choice and whether *you* feel it is right for the model in hand. One thing is for sure; there will be some clever person out there somewhere who will be pleased to tell you that you've got it wrong!

Instead of the black marker pen you can use matt black enamel. However, a far greater degree of care in application is required if paint isn't to be spread far and wide over the face of the plank, but it does have a different absorption rate into the edge of the timber and provides yet another subtle result.

Unfortunately, should your particular kit come with 0,5 - 0,6mm thick strips for deck planking, it is unlikely that the above methods will be available to you. Such thin material often cuts with a less than perfect edge; particularly if the grain is on the coarse side, and any attempt to blacken the edge will result in any faults being highlighted. The best answer in these circumstances is probably to forget trying to simulate caulking and merely butt the planks edge to edge.

Another procedure favoured by some modellers is the black thread method. Having positioned one plank, a length of black thread is laid taut along one edge and the next plank then positioned tightly against it. This works quite well once you have got used to making sure that the thread is completely down on to the deck throughout its length, and that you have chosen a thread diameter that is somewhat smaller than the plank thickness. Failure to recognise these conditions can cause a problem when you come to rub down the deck, since you don't want to rub down the top surface of the thread as well!

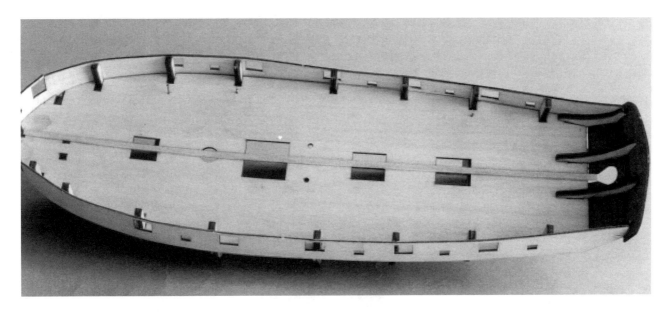

Fig. 7.3 Laying the first plank.

Preparing the Deck Planks

Many kits that provide for making just a representative model of the marque will merely indicate planking laid in strips from stem to stern. If, however, you wish to enhance the quality of your model, you can lay the deck with scale length planks in the true fashion and adopting the right pattern. A decision to do this requires a little research to determine the correct length of the planks for the vessel in question and to establish whether the laying pattern conforms to the four-butt shift, or the three-butt shift, system. This decides whether there are three or four planks between butt joints on the same frame or bulkhead, **Fig.7.2**.

If you have decided to "caulk" the deck by marking one or both edges of the planking strips, it is better to do this before cutting the strips up into the shorter lengths. It is not usually necessary to caulk the ends of the cut planks since, when cut with a scalpel or other type of knife, the edge is turned over sufficient to throw

Fig. 7.4 Missing the hatches.

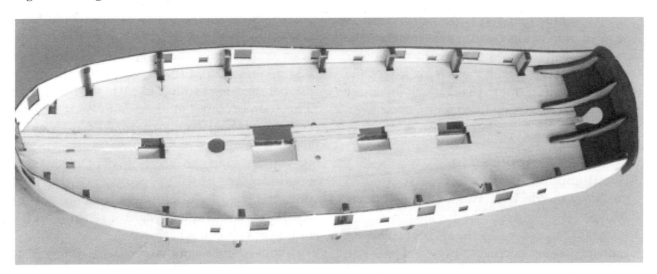

Fig. 7.5 Finished, straightforward planking with no butts.

a shadow that is adequate to delineate the butt joints.

While it is not usual to find severe variations in the thickness of strips supplied for deck planking, it is well worth taking a few minutes to have a check so that any rogue piece can be put to one side. Reducing the odd thick plank once the deck is laid is not too difficult, but reducing the whole deck to suit one or two thin planks is not as easy as might be first thought.

It is essential that all planks be of identical length or the laying pattern goes out of the window. I tend to use an Amati Mastercut tool for this operation purely because it makes the job simpler, but it doesn't take much ingenuity to make up a simple jig from scrap wood from the kit.

Application.

A word about adhesives before starting to actually lay the deck. If you are using a plank thickness less than 1mm then, almost certainly, a contact adhesive is best for the job. Cyanoacrylate is acceptable provided that you

are experienced enough to position things correctly first time. White PVA has the potential to warp the planks and raise their edges as it dries, and this makes the subsequent rubbing down process really difficult. However, its use on plank thickness of 1mm and above seems to work well.

The kit instructions will almost certainly advise that you start in the middle of the deck and work outwards towards the bulwarks. Irrespective of the fact that you may have chosen to lay the deck with a series of shorter, scale length planks, the first central plank should be one long strip, **Fig.7.3**, and left to properly dry before using a scalpel to cut in the butt joints. This then becomes in effect your master plank from which all the others will take their alignment.

If you are going to use butted planks, it is a good move to pencil the position of the butts onto the false deck before you actually start to lay the planks. This takes care of "losing" position at any opening in the deck.

Should there be any hatchways or other openings in the deck, try not to completely plank over them, even temporarily, but leave access to get a knife, scalpel or other cutting tool in so that they can be subsequently opened up to size, **Fig.7.4**.

When the planking reaches the bulwarks, some shaping of the outer planks will be necessary. However, bearing in mind my earlier point about not planking the inside of the bulwarks until after laying the deck, it will now be seen where the advantage lies. The degree of accuracy required to fit the outer deck planks to the bulwarks is reduced because the thickness of the inner bulwark planking will ultimately cover any small gaps left.

Margin planks are not usually a feature of kit-built models but there is no reason why, with a bit of research, they cannot be added to enhance the model. Now is the time to accommodate them should you so wish.

More rubbing down is in order now to get the deck surface clean and smooth. One tool that can be very effective is the single-edged razor blade used as a scraper. This more readily removes any local high spots and provides a nice flat surface. I usually apply a rubbed-in coat of shellac based sanding sealer to the deck before finishing-off with fine abrasive paper. This helps protect the surface during the ongoing construction of the model. If you use the razor blade method, fairly soon after gluing the planks down

to the false deck, you will find that the stroking action involved helps seat the planks firmly. A typical straightforward deck can be seen in **Fig.7.5**.

Hatches, companionways and any other apertures can now be trimmed to finished size before moving on to the next stage of the building process.

Inner Bulwark Planking

It is helpful, if required, to paint at least the first plank before seating it tight down onto the deck planking. This, as before, provides a hard line contrast between the two surfaces far more easily than painting afterwards.

It is usually advisable to plank slightly higher than the top line of the outer planking so that the line of the top of the bulwarks can be established simultaneously with them.

Soaking planks at the forward end is frequently necessary as an aid to bending. The plank nipper is not an option in this case because the exposed face of the plank is on the inside of the bend, where the nipper leaves its characteristic mark. However, some gentle tweaking with thumb and forefinger will usually suffice to introduce enough of a bend to put the plank in place, with small clamps or crocodile clips to finally pull the plank in tight to the inside of the bulwark.

Elbe, 545mm long from a Constructo kit.

CHAPTER EIGHT

Wales and Rails

The wales on a full-size man-of-war were those extra heavy-duty planks placed at strategic levels along the side of hull to provide additional fore and aft stiffness. They were fixed directly to the edges of the frames. This rarely happens in a kit and the wales planking is more often than not laid on top of the second planking. Rails were the much lighter features, more adjacent to the top of the bulwarks. Before fitting any of them, it is worth taking a look at the position of any quarter gallery castings or indeed, the stern fascia. Rails and wales often terminate or blend into features evident on these castings and it is absolutely essential that these terminations are at the same height on both sides of the hull, or the whole of the back end alignments can be thrown into trouble.

Fig. 8.1 Parallel wales on _H.M.S. Mars._

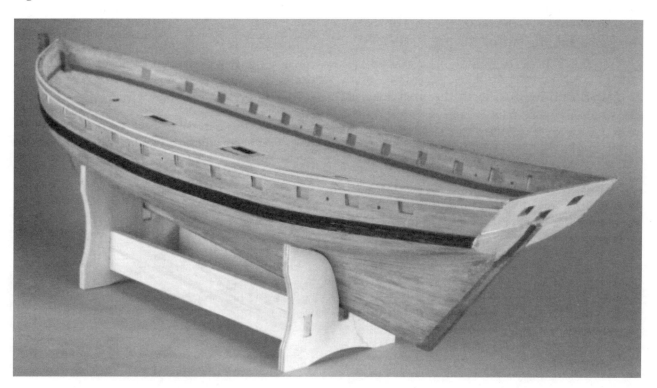

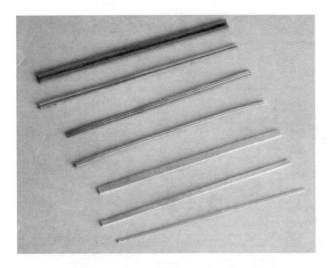

Fig. 8.2 Various sections of decorative wood and brass strip.

The Main Wale

The main wale, and on larger vessels, the upper wale, is usually constructed by laying several rows of planking side by side to make up the wide, and parallel, band of timber down the side of the hull. Position is all-important and attention should be given to ensure that they are put on at the right level and in identical position both sides. If the model has gun-ports these can often be guide points in determining the run of the wales, although remember that the alignments are not the same, the gun-ports being parallel to the line of the gun decks.

While it may seem completely irrelevant to think about painting at this stage of the build, it is worth noting that if, in the final analysis, the wales are to be painted, now is a good time to save yourself from the traumas of the shaking hand syndrome later on! Consider painting at least the edges of the top and bottom planks before assembly in order to attain a sharp crisp line against the unpainted side of the hull. In fact, this is a tip that can apply equally to all rails and wales.

Upper Wale and Rails

The same comments apply here as to the main wale. Additionally, it is worth checking on the drawings to see if these features run parallel to the top edge of the main wale. If they do, then it is worth making up a couple of distance pieces as gauges to ensure that these lesser wales run true. Sometimes the run of the upper rails relates to the top edge of the hull and, again, distance pieces of relevant width will prove useful, **Fig.8.1**.

Rails are frequently made from square sectioned strip which, when taken from the box, may have somewhat pronounced saw marks on at least two of their faces. Do remember to sand these off before the strips are glued to the hull. The marks may not be too noticeable in the natural wood, but show up quite alarmingly when painted.

Decorative rails may come in the form of rolled brass strips of relevant section and one enterprising manufacturer provides pre-cut ply strips of "U" section, **Fig.8.2**.

Irrespective of what form ornamental rails take, they are usually best put in place with cyanoacrylate. But do remember, even cyanoacrylate doesn't stick well to paint, so such surfaces should be appropriately prepared.

Bulwark Rails

I sometimes wonder whether some kit manufacturers ever make up a prototype model from the actual box of bits they sell to the public or, if they do, choose to ignore some of the problems they encounter. The average kit builder, and certainly the beginner, does not have the facility the bend strip material across its width. Yet there are occasions when the modeller is expected to do just that. My tip to those who

Fig. 8.3 Pre-cut bulwark capping rails with slots for timberheads.

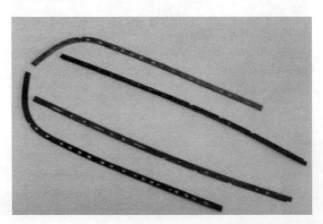

Fig. 8.4 Bow hair bracket and bow cheeks in place.

are faced with the problem is, "Don't even try; do it differently."

If you are lucky, there may be some ply sheet in the kit of the right thickness that has enough spare from which to cut the rails, if not, it is well worth the cost of buying a sheet. Lay the sheet flat on the bench, place the model hull deck down on to it and trace the outline of the top of the bulwarks with a pencil on to the ply. Depending on the thickness involved, use a craft knife or fretsaw to cut along the line and produce the outer edge of the rail. Now draw a second line inside, and parallel to the first, to indicate the required width of the rail, and carefully cut along this line to separate the rail from the sheet. What you have now is a rail that is of the exact shape to suit your model, with minimal adjustment being required for overhang, and no bending.

Some of the more recent kits provide pre-cut rails that conform to this basic pattern, **Fig.8.3** and, provided that you have constructed the hull shape correctly, you get an excellent result. Take care when the kit instructions advise mitred, or scarfed, joints to construct the rails from several pieces. This requires much greater precision and the pieces really do need to be well glued in place before final shaping. Not too difficult, but unnecessarily hazardous. An important point to remember when following this method is that you cannot make a specified width of rail from the same width of timber. No matter how many pieces you include into the curved rail, the width of strip used must always be wider than the finished rail.

Head Rails

As far as this part of the ship model goes, kits come in three classes, excellent, average and terrible.

One or two of the more enlightened kit manufacturers have recognised that the head rails of a period ship are one of the greater challenges of model making and have given considerable thought as to how best to aid the

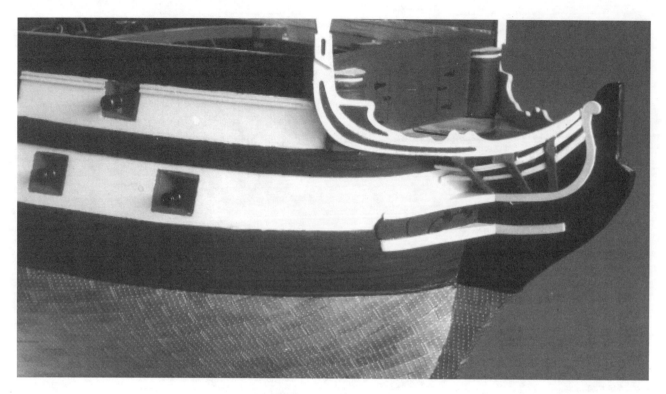

Fig. 8.5 Head rails and frames with bow main rails in position.

model maker. Resulting from their efforts and the specific use of computer aided design and manufacture, head rails for many models can now be built without having to perform intricate bending operations and the use of unseemly vocabulary, **Figs.8.4, 8.5** and **8.6**.

Most modern kits still expect the modeller to use a greater degree of handicraft to cut and bend strip and sheet to attain the necessary curves and shapes involved, albeit that the box may well contain helpful pliable beech wood. The terrible kits do not go even that far and the builder is faced with all sorts of problems in his attempts to get anywhere near the required shapes.

While it is impossible to examine here all the variations of curve and shape that the modeller can come across, there are some basic hints that may well pave the way to an easier outcome. The first important thing to remember, is that whatever is produced for the starboard side has to be reproduced, in the opposite hand, for the port side. Secondly, examination of the various parts that go to make up the whole will reveal that while some items may well have a fancy shape, they are nonetheless flat. These bits require the normal patience and fine working ability that most model makers have. Further examination of the drawing may indicate that there are some parts that could well be made in the same fashion although the instruction manual suggests the bent strip procedure. This would be a case for considering deviating from the kit recommended method. Finally you have the bent bits and, maybe even worse, parts that are compounded by curves in two planes. So, you don't worry about the flat bits, they may well tax your patience, but mostly it is a matter of time rather than downright difficulty. Let's look at the curved bits.

The provision of flexible beech strip will ease the problems considerably and, whether or not you are fortunate enough to find this material in your kit, the procedures will be basically the same if you have to contend with the less pliable material. You are almost certainly going to need some sort of bending equipment. It doesn't have to be more sophisticated than what is

Fig. 8.6 The cast decorative strip from the underside of the cathead bracket has been added.

essentially a soldering iron with a large cylindrical bit stuck on the end and a wooden shaped former that can be held in the vice.

Cut all the strip oversize on length and do the bending first, making two identical parts at a time one for starboard and one for port. Having got the curves right, the ends can be shaped to fit the sides of the hull or the prow of the vessel. Remember, that it is this treatment of the ends that determine the "hand" of the part, so while the physical dimensions remain the same, the chamfering and trimming is round the other way.

It is not a bad idea to take a short straight scrap length of strip and produce the end shapes to make sure that you have them the right way round. These can then be copied onto the bent parts with greater confidence. Do not despair if you initially make some wrong, we have all done it. In fact I have a small drawer of scrap,

bent pieces that I keep in case they might come in handy for my next model. They never seem to – but one day...

It is definitely worth painting all parts before assembly with at least two coats of paint, assuming of course, that a painted finish is required. Getting a brush into all the nooks and crannies of assembled head-rails is an absolute nightmare and pre-painting is undoubtedly the best procedure.

Having got all the parts made and painted to your satisfaction, don't rush the assembly. Leaving the glue holding the head timbers that fit laterally across the prow to set thoroughly before attempting to fit the curved rails in place.

I sincerely hope that, as time passes, more of the manufacturers will adopt the more helpful approach and that the days of intricate bending and bad language will become a thing of the past.

Le Renommee, 690mm long, from a Euromodel Como kit

CHAPTER NINE

The Stern and Quarter Galleries

Now to work on the other end of the ship, where alignments are just as critical. It is usual that any back-plate or stern fascia, whether they be wooden or cast, be fitted first either temporarily or permanently to provide alignment points for fitting the quarter galleries, stern galleries, or any other of the fancy ornamentation that was frequently featured on these old period ships. Should the kit design decree that, for some reason or another, the quarter galleries should be fitted first, then the relative height of salient features, port and starboard must be absolutely identical. Failure to achieve this state will be most evident to the eye when fitting the stern gallery and, thereafter, when viewing the stern of the completed model.

Handling Castings

On earlier produced kits, one of the major problems was trying to induce curves into flat castings that were made from metal and really did not want to bend! Fortunately, castings today are generally cast in a softer material. However, they still need a gentle touch and a lot of patience if success is to be achieved. Try to creep up on the final curve required and avoid overbending so that you have to come back to it. This stresses the material, can cause cracks and, in the case of some more fragile parts, complete breakage. In the majority of cases, the thumbs and fingers can be the best tools; the feel of the material moving can be better sensed than if you put the part into a vice and use a pair of tongs!

Cast faces that have to mate with the surfaces on the hull will probably need some adjustment to get a nice snug fit, as will mating faces between adjacent castings. These adjustments are a matter of patience rather than serious difficulty and well-cleaned files should be adequate for the job. For those readers not familiar with the techniques of filing, a file needs to be kept clear of residual material trapped in its teeth. A file card, or small wire brush, will normally remove the offending pieces but, be removed they must, or they will possibly gouge lumps out of the surface you are trying to shape.

Depending on the age and condition of the moulds in which the castings are formed, will be the degree of cleaning up the castings will require. Difficulties can arise in two forms; the first being *excessive flash* and the second, more problematical, being *offset*. Flash occurs when the two parts of the mould fail to properly come together, leaving a line of residual material around the cast part. This line can always be seen even on the best quality castings and can normally be removed very easily. Excessive, thick flash is undesirable and, by definition, indicates an oversize part. Offset is the result of the two parts of the mould not coming together accurately and in true alignment. This

Fig. 9.2 Simulated glazing on *H.M.S. Bellona.*

Fig. 9.1 Open framed cast parts suitable for glazing

often results in the casting being totally useless, since the condition cannot be corrected by filing, without the part becoming misshapen or undersized. Referral back to the manufacturer is usually the best course of action with a request for a replacement.

Again depending upon the way the cast parts have been produced, you may find that there is some residue of a mould release agent. A scrub over with an old toothbrush and some washing-up liquid is thus an advisable operation before proceeding further and involving adhesives and paint.

Glazing

If open frames are a feature of the gallery castings or other inboard facias, then thought should be given to glazing the windows, **Fig.9.1**. More recently introduced kits actually provide recesses behind the windows to accept pieces of clear, acetate sheet cut to the appropriate size. Should castings with open frames not have such re-

cesses, small pieces of cling-film may be used between the casting and the wooden surface onto which it is mounted. Cling-film is fiddly to use but, being very thin, does not interfere with the glued joint like the thicker, acetate sheet. A somewhat controversial matter relates to the colour that should be used to paint the surface behind the glazing. Look across the road to your neighbours' houses and I doubt if you see white, silver or blue windows; all colours that I have seen specified in kit instructions at one time or another. The safest colour to use is, in my opinion, either matt black or matt dark grey; matt being used because the overlying film of glazing material is reflective anyway. The paint should be applied to the wooden surface onto which the casting is to be mounted and not onto the back of the film.

If the castings do not feature open, framed windows, then glazed surfaces should be simulated with gloss paint, using dark grey as first choice. **Fig. 9.2** illustrates such a result.

Fig. 9.4 Finishing off the *San Felipe's* stern with railings and decoration.

Adhesives

Any of the two part epoxy products should be suitable and for larger castings, at least, preferable to thick cyanoacrylate. Three rules should be observed when using this class of adhesive, thoroughly mix, use the correct proportions, and don't mix any more than you need. The last may not sound too important, but the danger lies in the temptation to use it all up without remembering glue that is "going off" does not stick properly.

Application

It is imperative that the drawings provided are studied most carefully before trying to permanently assemble any of the parts that go to make up what is sometimes a most complex construction. The instruction manual is often a bit lacking when it comes to adequately describing this part of the building process and the modeller may well be left largely to his own devices to decide on sequences and procedures.

It is generally useful to keep a steel rule to hand, or even a pair of dividers or inside

callipers, in order to maintain checks on relative positions, port and starboard.

Most of the fitting work involved in building up the quarter and stern galleries comprises a lot of patience and gentle trial and error procedures, constantly offering up tweaked parts until the required fit is attained. It is frequently advisable to let the adhesive thoroughly set before moving on to the next stage in order that things do not get disturbed when building one piece upon another. The golden rule is to be absolutely certain that you have got each bit right before you finally glue it in place.

Painting and glazing prior to the assembly of parts may well prove beneficial, if not essential, so it is wise to always keep in mind the content of the next stage of construction as well as the overall picture.

Remember too that some of the gallery decks may be partially exposed behind railings and that these should be planked and finished before putting such railings in place, **Figs. 9.3 and 9.4**.

Decoration frequently consists of castings of leaf-work, mermaids, cherubs and the like,

Fig. 9.5 Decoration on the *Royal Caroline.*

sitting on a painted background, **Fig. 9.5**.

These are often complex shapes; don't stick them on and *then* try painting the background round them - do the background first, then glue them on.

Do not forget that glue does not adhere well to paint; scrape an area of paint away so that your cherubs don't fall off overnight.

CHAPTER TEN

Gun Ports

One of the most critical aspects of introducing gun-ports into the side of the hull is getting them in the right place. Some of the more recent kits on the market feature preformed, ply upper-works for the first planking that includes the apertures for the guns, **Fig.10.1**. Provided that these ply pieces are correctly positioned at the commencement of the hull construction, then the marking out process is not a problem. However, the majority of kits demand that the

model-maker has to do the task and handle the associated problems. So, what are the difficulties? Obviously, getting them in the right place, all in the right attitude and all the same size.

Position

The line of the gun ports is relative to the line of the relevant gun deck on which the guns are mounted. They *do not* follow the line of the wales

Fig. 10.1 Pre-cut gun-ports for *H.M.S. Mars.*

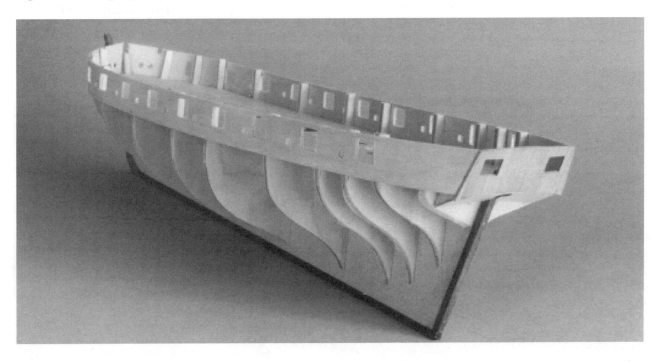

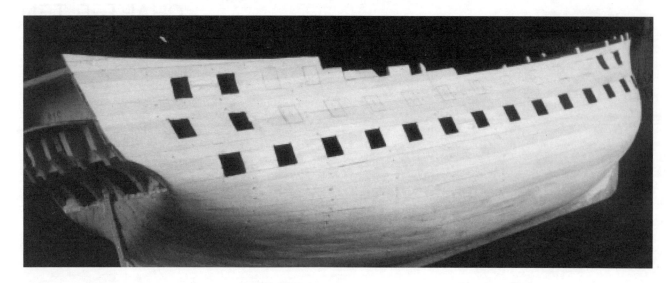

Fig. 10.2 Marked and cut gun-ports on *H.M.S. Bellona.*

because it makes them more pleasing to the eye! If, as hull construction proceeded, you had maintained adequate reference to the levels of the gun decks featuring false barrels, then defining the level of the relevant row of gun-ports will be that much easier.

For gun-ports relating to decks where carriage guns or carronades are exposed, a useful dodge is to make up one of the gun assemblies and use it as a gauge to determine the correct height of the gun-port aperture above deck level.

Size and Attitude

Getting all the apertures to the same size is important because any odd one, be it slightly larger or a bit smaller than its mates, stands out like a sore thumb. In order to minimise the difficulties the following procedures are most effective. First determine what the actual size of the gun-port should be and make a template by cutting an aperture of that size in a piece of stiff card or plasticard. Position a strip of masking tape along the hull to coincide with the bot-

Fig. 10.3 Lined and painted gun-ports on *H.M.S. Bellona.*

tom edge of the gun-ports then, using this as a guide, run a pencil around the inside of the template at every gun-port position, making sure that all vertical sides are indeed vertical. On many vessels, towards the stern, the lower sills of the gun-port will cut into the top of the main wale; make sure that the alignment of the masking tape is kept true where this happens.

As to the size of the aperture in the template, this will depend on whether or not the ports are cut through the planking at finished size and the end grain of the two layers of planking finished smooth or, whether the gun-ports are to be lined. If the latter condition applies, then the aperture in the template should be enlarged on height and width by twice the thickness of the relevant lining material. Such ports are shown in **Fig.10.2** cut into the first planking of *H.M.S. Bellona.*

Cutting Out

The creating of the gun-port is far simpler if the hull construction featured preformed apertures from the word go, it being merely necessary to trim the ends of the combined first and second planking out to the required size. Unfortunately, not too many kits have progressed this far as yet and, thus, the majority of gun-ports have to be introduced in the time-honoured fashion using drills, knives and files.

Having marked out the shape and position of the aperture, the normal way to remove the middle is to first drill all round inside the outline, so that each hole just overlaps its neighbour, then trim and file the resultant jagged edge until you reach the desired outline. However, there are some snags to trap the unwary.

First of all consider the drill size; if you choose a drill that is too small you are going to have to drill a far greater number of holes and, if your model calls for eighty or more gun-ports, you are going to be in for a lengthy session of drilling. On the other hand, selecting a larger diameter drill can reduce the drilling content of the operation, but then you need to watch the *break-out* factor. This is the damage caused where the drill breaks through the inner planking. It may not be too much of a problem where the lower gun decks are concerned, but care is needed where inner surfaces are exposed to the eye on the finished model. There are two significant things that can be done to help overcome the difficulty, keep the drill sharp and start the drilled hole a little further inside the finished outline.

When trimming out the aperture, maintain sharp blades in knife or scalpel and, in the case of expose,d inner surfaces, try and trim the edges of the gun-ports from both sides, the final sizing being best done with a file. As was stated before, getting all ports to the same size is important and a small, plug gauge made up from scrap timber is a useful means to this end. It is usually easier to finish two adjacent sides square and position by eye, then work on the two opposite sides to attain final size using the plug gauge.

Lining

Lining the gun-ports gives a much more professional look to the model. The vertical sides are put in first to full aperture height, followed by the upper and lower sills. The strip material used for this lining is normally wide enough to overhang the inner and outer faces of the hull in order to accommodate the tumblehome, or angular surface on the outside of the planking. Excess material can then be trimmed off flush when glue has thoroughly set. Lined gun-ports in *H.M.S. Bellona* are shown in **Fig.10.3**.

With some models that are to a larger scale and therefore more detailed, the front edges of the lining pieces may be set back from the surface of the hull in order to form a recess into which the gun-port lid can sit. Fitting such lining pieces is not difficult, but they do require to be shaped on their outer edges prior to gluing in place.

The inner, bulwark planking and the inside surfaces of the gun-port lining are frequently painted dark red, even when the finished model is predominantly left in natural wood. It is certainly easier to do this before mounting dummy gun barrels or assembled carriage guns and carronades.

Fig. 10.4 Port lids and tackle on *H.M.S. Agamemnon.*

Gun-Port Lids

These may well be the subject of pre-cut parts, which will require only to be cleaned up on the edges, before assembling with hinges and maybe, eyebolts. Many kits however, will expect the modeller to fabricate the basic lids from strip material. This usually involves sticking two pieces together edge to edge to form a sufficiently wide piece. It saves much time and agony if two full-length strips are so put together, left overnight for the glue to properly cure then the individual lids cut off to the required length with a razor saw.

Lids are usually made up of two plies, the inner one being a little smaller than the outer in order to fit inside the port lining, the outer fitting in the aforementioned recess. The inner ply may be made in the same manner as the outer.

Hinges may be provided in the kit as cast, pressed brass, or photo-etched parts. In all cases they should be painted before assembly and every endeavour made to stick them in the same positions on every gun-port lid.

Fitting the lids to the sides of the hull is entirely dependant upon the design of the hinges. These normally come in one of two forms, the purely decorative, in which case the fitting of the lid is an edge gluing exercise or, the hinge with a rear spigot that involves drilling holes into the hull to accept the spigots and, for safety, edge gluing as well.

Eyebolts may be required at the front edge of each lid to take the port tackle. See later notes in *Chapter Eleven* about preparing and fitting of eyebolts to best advantage.

Whether you choose to mount the lids at this time, or leave then until later, is a matter of personal choice. When fitted, it should be remembered that they have to be rigged with what can be seen of the port tackle, ropes that come through the hull sides down to the front edge of the lids, **Fig.10.4**.

An effective way of rigging this tackle is to drill holes into the side of the hull at the appropriate places, then taking a length of thread, smear one end with cyanoacrylate to form a bodkin. When stiffened, apply a further touch of cyanoacrylate and push well into the hole in the side of the hull and when set, lash the other end to an eyebolt in the front edge of the lid, keeping the thread as taut as possible.

CHAPTER ELEVEN

Fitting Out

As a complete change to the heavier work of hull construction, we can now consider all the add-on bits most of which sit on the deck or somewhere around the outside of the hull. Some of these sub-assemblies can be treated like mini-projects and, in fact, many modellers make things like anchors and capstans as a bit of light relief during some of the more tedious and long-winded tasks, like planking for instance.

In many kits, these items come from standard listings of fittings and, as such, sometimes fall into the category of "near enough." Near enough the right size and near enough the right shape! However there is, thankfully, a growing trend to provide kits with fittings dedicated to the vessel in hand. This is good news for those model makers who want to get their model historically correct. Anchors, capstans and pumps are typical of the "standard" items concerned.

Probably the most significant failing of the model maker in this part of the build is a lack of adequate fixing. It has to be remembered that many items will come under load during the later rigging process and that is definitely not the time when you want bits to fall off, pull off, or generally fall apart because insufficient attention has been given to the task of fixing them in the first place. This chapter will constantly refer to the importance of fixing so that, hopefully, at least some readers will not go through the trauma of having to remove rigging and re-glue parts, before starting again.

The sequence of making and assembling the various items to be fitted onto the hull and deck will largely depend on the particular model in hand. In the majority of cases it is wise to stick to the sequence indicated in the instruction manual. The following list is in alphabetical order provides a brief understanding of what each item does, and highlights things that the modeller should, perhaps, pay particular attention to.

Anchors
Used for holding and retaining the ship. They normally comprised an iron shank with a pair of flukes or palms at the lower end and a large ring at the top. Immediately below the ring, and at right angles to the line of the flukes, the anchor was fitted with a wooden stock, the function of the stock being to guide the flukes to be perpendicular with the seabed.

In kits, the shank and flukes are usually integrally cast parts, with the stock being made from one or two pieces of timber. The cast parts should be cleaned up to remove flash, then painted matt black. The stock should be made to fit the top of the shank snugly and, before fixing in place, fitted with either iron bands or rope lashings, depending upon the period

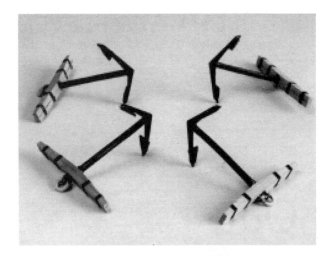

Fig. 11.1 Anchors. Note puddening on rings and the iron bands simulated by black cartridge paper.

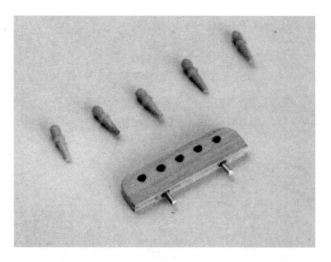

Fig. 11.2 Pin rails for inside the bulwarks. Note the locating pins.

concerned. Lashings are, of course, done in a suitable size of thread, and narrow strips of black cartridge paper can simulate iron bands. Use PVA to stick the cartridge paper, but remember that because the underside of the stock is usually tapered, you cannot go all round the stock in one go. Do the top and two sides with one piece, adding the bottom piece separately.

The ring should be fitted after the stock has been put in place. It is worth taking the trouble to add the protective covering called "puddening." This is done by winding around the ring with, say, 0,5mm diameter rigging thread. This is one of those features frequently not mentioned in the instruction manual, but one that adds a bit of class to the finished model, **Fig.11.1**.

Belaying Pin Rails or Racks

In some cases these have to be fabricated from a suitable size strip, in others they come preformed within a ply sheet, complete with holes ready to mount belaying pins. If they have to be fabricated from strip, it is worth considering marking out the positions of the holes for all the rails required, centre-popping each position with a sharp scriber and drilling them all together before cutting them of into separate rails. Choose a drill size that is the same as the diameter of the belaying pin shank, just

below its head. This permits the maximum length of shank to protrude below the rack, a condition that will be appreciated later during the rigging process.

The fixing of these items to the inside of the bulwarks is one that needs at least two pin fixings to supplement the adhesive. Choose positions fairly near the ends of the rail and between holes previously drilled to take the belaying pins and, depending on the thickness of the rail, select a suitable diameter of brass wire to make the dowel pins. Drill holes the same size as the wire diameter into the chosen positions in the back edge of the rails and glue in a short length of the wire. Cut the protruding length back as required **Fig.11.2**.

The rail should now be offered up to the inside of the hull in order to mark the position of *one* of the pins. Using a pin vice and drill, merely start the hole in the hull. Position the rail again inserting one pin into the partially drilled hole and use the end of the other pin to mark its position. Both holes can now be fully drilled, taking care not to go right through the hull. The back edge of the rail can now be glued, together with the pins, and put into place on the inside of the hull. Don't forget to scrape off any paint from the gluing area first.

Having dealt with the racks that fit around the insides of the bulwarks, we can now turn to those that sit around the bottom of the masts.

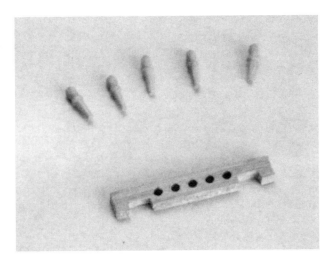

Fig. 11.3 Post mounted pin rails.

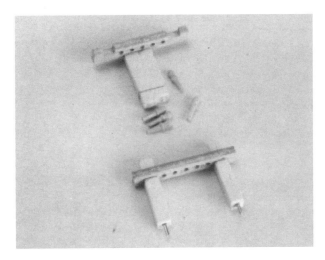

Fig. 11.4 Dry assemble all posts to rails to establish identical heights.

The rails with the belaying pin holes are made in the same way as described above, with the exception of the locating pins in the rear edges. This time they are jointed into posts that are, in turn, glued and pinned into the deck. The joints concerned are simple notches in the posts into which are glued the rails, **Fig.11.3**.

The only significant problem in making the posts is getting the slots all the same height above deck level. Try cutting the posts over-length, making the slots in approximately the right place and dry assembling one of the rails across all the posts concerned with the specific assembly in hand, **Fig.11.4**. With the rail in place,

the bottom of all the posts can now be established at the same time, a similar process then being employed for the tops.

As mentioned above, the posts should be fixed to the deck using a pin or dowel made from 1mm or 1,5mm brass wire.

Many modellers find it helpful not to assemble the belaying pins at this juncture but fit them as required when doing the rigging.

Bitts

These consisted of two, stout, vertical posts with a horizontal beam, designed and positioned

Fig. 11.5 Bitts at the foremast on *H.M.S. Agamemnon*. See also the catheads.

Fig. 11.6 Capstan and elmtree pumps fabricated from cast and pre-cut parts. Note the pins to aid fixing in the bottom of the pumps.

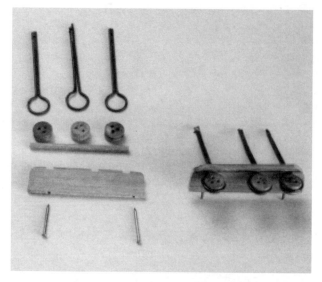

Fig. 11.7 Wire deadeye strops glued into channels and capped.

to take the strain of holding the anchor cables when the ship was riding at anchor; the posts would be further supported by brackets on their forward side above deck. Passing through each deck below, they would be bolted to the deck beams and eventually be housed in the keelson.

The kit builder will normally be concerned only with that part of the bitt system that shows above the deck and the only problems that are likely to arise are in making sure that the beam is horizontally jointed into the post and that the posts are firmly dowelled into the deck, **Fig.11.5**. These potential difficulties can be overcome in the same manner as that described for the posts supporting the pin racks and rails.

Capstans

There are several different designs of capstan available, any one of which may feature in your kit. The most common is that with turned core, base and top, requiring the addition of preformed whelps. The problem that is frequently found with this type is that the whelps are grossly undersize and need to be remade in order to fit properly between base and top. The final appearance is also improved if trouble is taken to ensure that they are assembled equally spaced around the core.

Some kits provide a more refined capstan

assembled from a series of pre-cut parts. These afford a higher degree of detail, even to the provision of square holes for the capstan bars, **Fig.11.6**.

Capstan bars, made from scrap timber, lashed up and stowed on deck are an enhancement that may be considered or, alternatively, may be inserted into the capstan head ready for use. Similarly, and if pertinent, a simulation of the pawls for the ratchet system is something that adds a bit of class to the model.

Fig. 11.8 Etched brass strops with locking prongs.

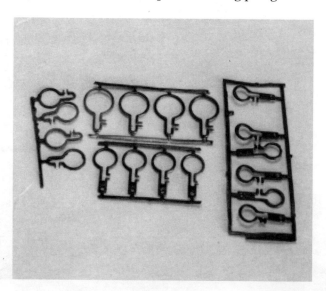

Catheads

These beams passed through the bulwarks at the bow of the ship and were angled forward, usually on a radial line from the centre of the foremast. They were normally supported externally by a large bracket, from their undersides onto the side of the hull. Sheaves at the outer end, helped to hoist the anchor from the water and also to keep it clear from the side of the hull when dropping anchor, (Refer back to **Fig.11.5**.

It is often required that the modeller cut a square hole through the bulwarks to take the cathead. This can be done in the same manner as used for a gun-port, at all times recognising the angles involved to achieve a snug fit. The cathead itself should be drilled with the appropriate number of holes to simulate the sheaves. The inner end will normally be angled on its underside so that it seats well on the deck and adopts the correct angle poking out from the front of the bows.

The cathead brackets are handed due to the angles on their back edge that should fit tight against the outside of the hull.

Channels and Deadeye Strop

The channels are fixed to the hull following the same procedure as that described for the pin rails, although one major difference is the

Fig. 11.9 Various styles of chain plate systems.

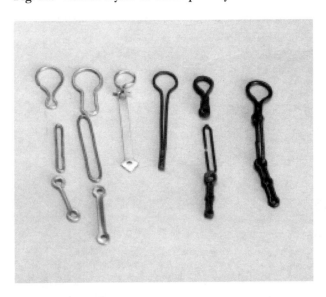

curve on the back edge of the channels. For the best possible joint, this curve should be checked to match that on the side of the hull and adjusted accordingly. Depending upon the design of the deadeye strops and the personal preference of the modeller, deadeyes may be fixed to the channels before or after assembly to the outside of the hull.

It is usual for the bottom end of the deadeye strops to locate into slots cut in the edge of the channels, then be retained by a capping strip. In many cases, the strops, each fitted with a deadeye, merely drop into the slot and rely on being properly glued to prevent "pull-out." **Fig.11.7**. Two-part epoxy is the best choice of adhesive, ensuring that a correctly mixed and fresh batch is used.

With the advent of photo-etched strops, one now sometimes finds a built-in, locking device designed specifically to prevent "pull-out." **Fig.11.8**. Here, the deadeye is loaded into the strop, (correct orientation please), and locking prongs are sprung into one of the back corners of each slot in the edge of the channel. Although I have tested the system on several occasions and have never been able to pull the strop out of the channel, using normal rigging tension, I still put a blob of adhesive in the channel slot before adding the capping strip. Call it 'belt and braces' if you will, but if you have ever experienced the problems that can arise if deadeyes pull out of channels when rigging lower shrouds, or mast tops when rigging upper shrouds, you will appreciate the desire to make sure that it does not happen again.

Channels may also have eyebolts in their top surface. Bearing in mind the thickness of the channel material, it is probably best to leave the eyebolt shanks full length and, as well as using glue, bend the protruding part up tight under the bottom surface of the channel to prevent "pull-out."

Any knees required fitting between the upper surface of the channel and the side of the hull should now be put in place.

Chain Plates

These refer to the system of links that run from the bottom of the deadeye strop down to the

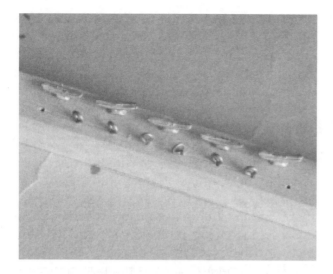

Fig. 11.10 Cleats and eyebolts in block ready for painting.

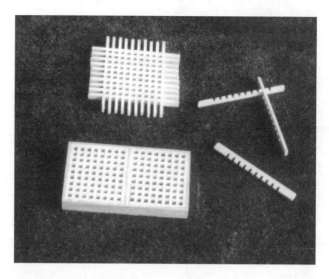

Fig. 11.11 Gratings.

hull. Historically, there are a number of designs to consider although only a few are likely to be found in kits. The amount of work that the modeller may have to do varies enormously depending on the quality of the kit. It might be relatively straightforward work like the assembly of photo-etched brass parts or preformed wire links, or the more tedious fabrication of wire shapes from scratch, starting with a plain piece of wire. The various options are seen in **Fig.11.09**.

The latter situation calls for a little bit of ingenuity to ensure that consistency of shape and size is attained. Formers made from scrap timber will frequently fill the need provided that the wire is sufficiently soft.

Whatever way in which the chain plates have to be made, their fixing to the hull needs a little care to ensure that the correct alignment is attained. Predominantly, although not exclusively, the line of the links follows that of the shroud with which they are associated. By far the easiest way to get this right is to assemble the links together and to the lower deadeye strop. Then, putting the end of a scriber or other such pointed tool into the hole of the lowest link, put tension on the system and guide into the correct alignment and mark the hull with the point of the scriber. Drill an undersize hole in the hull and push fit and glue a pin in place.

Chess Trees and Fenders

Chess trees were pieces of timber bolted to the hull used for bringing the main tack inboard and are best glued and pinned. Usually fabricated from appropriate sized strip material and requiring cut-a-ways on the back edge, they may also feature in the kit as pre-cut parts.

Fenders similarly fitted on the outside of the hull and were basically vertical skids for when hoisting the ship's boats inboard. Again, will normally be made from strip material and shaped to follow the exterior shape of the hull from the top of the main wale to the bulwark

Fig. 11.12 A combination of etched brass parts and castings make these lanterns for *H.M.S. Agamemnon*.

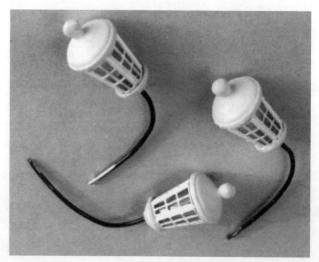

rail and be pinned and glued in place. May come in the kit as pre-cut parts.

Columns and Stanchions

Brass, boxwood or walnut is the material normally chosen for these turned parts used for building balustrades. There is a wide range of designs and sizes available and, provided the kit gives you enough, there really isn't too much to say about them. The main thing to watch for when fitting, are any little pips, left on the top or bottom from the parting off process. These should, of course, be removed to provide totally, flat ends.

Deck Cleats

These mainly cast parts merely require a drilled hole for fitting, but because of their more robust nature, the drill size selected can be the same as the shank or spigot, thus providing a gentle push fit. A similar, dry push fit into a piece of scrap timber permits a large quantity to be painted, at the same time, keeping the spigots free of paint, **Fig.11.10**.

Eyebolts

In the main, eyebolts, or shanked eyelets, are used as points for tying on rigging blocks, or termination points to which some parts of the rigging are lashed. They are the simplest form of fitting usually found in kits. They come in a variety of eye sizes and shank lengths and are usually made of copper or brass wire, generally polished, which is why the first job to be considered is to paint them matt black. I have a piece of scrap timber into which is drilled with a number of holes that nicely house the shanks of eyebolts right up to the underside of the eye. I load all of those supplied with the kit into those holes and give them a quick spray with black paint, (Refer again to **Fig.11.10**). The eyebolts are then taken out as they are needed having a black eye and a clean shank ready for fixing.

A drill size should be selected that is about 0,1mm larger than the shank of the eyebolt. You certainly don't want to try for a push fit or you will probably bend the shank trying to get it in,

or worse, damage the surface into which you are fixing. On the other hand you don't want to be able to throw the shank in from a couple of metres away or you will finish up with a weak joint; a hole 0,1mm larger is just about right.

Cyanoacrylate is satisfactory for fixing and a small pool dribbled out onto an old glazed dish is ideal to dip the shank of the eyebolt into before inserting it into the hole. Get the orientation of the eye correct and leave until cured. Get this latter positioning done fairly quickly or you can finish up with a "cold" joint.

Davits

In some vessels these were simply beams, similar to Catheads, hung over the ship's stern or quarters for hoisting and suspending the ship's boats. Like catheads they were furnished with sheaves or other appropriate tackle. From the modeller's point of view, simple to make but should be well fixed.

Gratings and Ladders

The kit invariably provides cross-halved, slotted strips to assemble and frame to make the gratings, **Fig.11.11**. The quality of these strips is all important to the success of making these deck parts and they should be examined particularly for constant and identical thickness; certainly any with taper should be discarded. If some are found to be thinner or thicker than others, then unless the difference is really extreme, they can be grouped together and kept for use to construct the same grating. The difference will probably not be noticed in that case but one odd strip in one grating will stand out.

Dry fit strips together, sufficient to cover the area of the grating required, remembering that when looking down onto the top surface, the edges of the battens, which can be totally seen, run fore and aft. The ledges, which are only apparent between the battens, run across the vessel, a point worthy of note, particularly for those entering competitions, or simply wishing to get as much right as possible.

Brush the assembled strips with diluted PVA and leave to dry; trim edges to final size. Cut the front and back frame pieces slightly over-length and glue them in place; trim ends to match width of unframed grating. Cut side frame pieces over-length and glue in place, trim off and finish all over with abrasive paper.

Vessels of later periods sometimes had hatch gratings with a convex top surface so a check should be made to see whether this is something that should be done before assembling the grating to the deck.

Ladders are not too difficult to make, but nonetheless, there are one or two points that are worthy of mention. The design is basically the same in all kits, two handed and slotted sidepieces plus a series of individual steps of identical length. The variation that you sometimes see is in the material chosen for the sides. Solid wood presents few problems but pre-formed parts routed in ply will frequently bend when removed from the sheet due to the stresses resulting from the slotting process being released. This is not a disastrous situation if you adopt a simple assembly procedure.

Use cyanoacrylate throughout to put the parts together and start by assembling the top and bottom steps into the sidepieces. Almost immediately, slide a third step into slots around the middle of the ladder and gently squeeze the sides inwards, and hold until the glue has set. The remainder of the steps can now be introduced. A similar procedure can, of course be adopted for the ladders with solid wooden sides, but the assembly of the third step in the middle of the ladder is not so critical to the ease of construction.

Lanterns

The Italian based kit manufacturers have a host of designs in their standard listings of accessories and it is from these that lanterns are usually drawn for inclusion in kits. They are generally highly detailed and probably better than the average modeller could make, so there isn't too much to say about them, except that sometimes the selection doesn't quite fit the period. You certainly don't want 17th century Spanish lanterns on the back of 18th century English ships of the line!

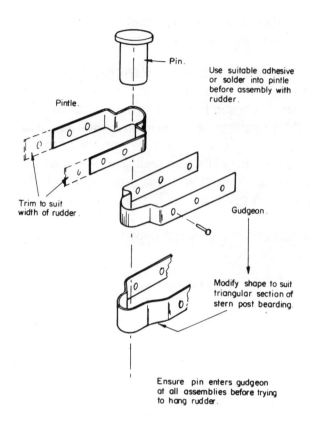

Fig. 11.13 Rudder Hinges.

One English manufacturer provides lanterns comprising a turned or cast top and bottom, separated by an etched brass body bent to shape by the modeller. These are designed and dedicated to the vessel concerned and, with the addition of a small piece of clear plastic rolled up to suit, look totally authentic, **Fig.11.12**.

The real problem with lanterns is in their mounting. Do not drill holes into the back of the model that are too big and hope that the glue will hold. Choose the smallest drill that will just allow the spigot or wire mounting to enter. It is often best to assemble the lantern with its main or central mounting first then add any subsidiary braces afterwards.

Pumps

Again, there are several "standard" designs available for kit manufacturers to draw on, some cast and some in wood that need to be assembled, **Fig.11.06**. Castings should be well fettled before painting and all completed pump units

Fig. 11.14 Ships wheel and "A" frames on *H.M.S. Cruiser.*

should be dowelled to the deck. There always seems to be something that draws inquisitive fingers to the pump handle to see if it goes up and down and, if it does, it will eventually do so once too often and the whole lot may get knocked off if not well secured!

Rudders

The making and fitting of the rudder is not necessarily the simple task that appearances lead you to believe, particularly if there are perhaps four or five hinges to contend with.

The hinge comprised the pintle and the gudgeon, the former being the piece with the pin that fitted on the rudder, and the latter being the item with the hole that was fixed to the rudder-post on the back of the hull and below the level of the pintle. For the rudder to be efficient, the gap between the front of the rudder and the post needed to be as small as possible. To that end, the entire hinge unit was housed in slots in the front edge of the rudder, those slots also being long enough to facilitate hoisting the pintles out of the gudgeons should the occasion demand.

The hinges included in kits fall mainly into two groups; those that are two pressed brass straps accompanied by a brass pin, **Fig.11.13**, and, the more authentic looking, that have straps

that are used in conjunction with turned, or cast, pintles and gudgeons.

The rudder blade is frequently pre-cut, but may not have the hinge slots prepared, in which case these need to be carefully spaced and cut in position. The front edges of the rudder should be rounded and a check made to see if there should be a taper, not only from front to back, but also from top to bottom. If the hull bottom has been copper plated, then the chances are that the rudder will also need to have its lower portion covered.

The pintles and straps should then be fitted making sure that all the pins are in line when viewed from both the front and the side. Cyanoacrylate can be used to assemble the straps and, when set, holes can be drilled into the rudder blade to take the fixing "bolts." These are made using dome headed pins cut off very short and stuck in position with a dab of cyanoacrylate.

Ultimately, the movement of the rudder will probably be limited by rudder chains that are fixed to spectacle bolts (use two eyebolts), at the top of the rudder blade and which run to either side of the stern plate. The addition of these is best left until much later in the construction of the model.

At the top end of the rudder was the tiller. This bar either passed through, or fixed over, the rudder stem and was the means by which it could be moved, from side to side, from inboard the vessel. On small ships it may have been a simple bar, which could be handled by a single helmsman without mechanical aid. On larger vessels the movement may have required the advantage of a system of ropes and blocks, operated by the ship's wheel.

I normally fix the rudder firmly to the model so that there is no movement at all. I do this on the basis that if something is suspected of being moveable, then attempts will be made to move it, with the consequent risk of breaking it. This is known as the "Inquisitive Finger Syndrome," see also the section on pumps.

The Ship's Wheel

Fitted to larger vessels, this was the visible end of the ship's steering mechanism. It varied somewhat in design from being a single or a double wheel but would be the means of rotating a drum, which would operate the rope and block system that was attached to the tiller.

The wheels supplied in kits are either standard wooden parts of roughly the correct diameter and usually of heavy and bulky appearance, or dedicated castings providing a more delicate shape with the correct number of spokes.

The wheel or wheels rotate a drum and together are supported by a pair of "A" frames or trunnions, **Fig.11.14**. In many models, this is all that is seen, which is a pity, because with the addition of a length of thread being wound around the drum with the ends passing down through the deck, the item becomes transformed and complete. On models of some smaller vessels, the rope system with its several blocks can be seen above deck and is something that the modeller will need to rig in the proper fashion.

The frames that support the wheel should, if possible, be dowelled to the deck. I usually make a point of fixing the wheel and drum to the frames so that they cannot rotate for the same reason that my rudders and pump handles don't move.

Side Steps

These may be made from one or two lengths of strip material or possibly be provided as pre-cut parts. If being cut from the strip, make sure that they are of equal length and, more importantly, are mounted on the side of the hull equally spaced and in line. Getting them correctly spaced is not difficult using a spacer cut from scrap. The edge of a strip of drafting tape stuck vertically on the hull side will provide an adequate marker for getting the ends of the steps in line.

Windlass

A lifting device similar in use to a capstan, but comprising a horizontal drum usually mounted across the fore part of the vessel where, due to its length, a greater number of men could assist in its operation. Sizes and styles vary enormously and the kit-builder is usually given pre-formed wooden or cast parts to assemble or, where greater attention to accuracy has been given by the manufacturer, pre-cut parts to build a more detailed unit. Whatever the provision, the need for secure fixing remains.

Other Miscellaneous Fittings

In today's kits, the use of photo-etched brass parts is increasing and it is now becoming possible to super-detail models to a standard hitherto unattainable by the modeller with only normal domestic facilities. Hooks, chain plate links, boarding pikes and a host of other items, formerly omitted under the claim of model makers' license, are now becoming the accepted norm. A typical sheet of parts can be seen by referring back to the photograph in *Chapter One*. This evolution does of course bring new techniques for the modeller to master.

Probably the most important of these is to successfully remove the part from the etched frame. A fairly hard surface to cut on is advisable and also a reasonably stout blade to actually separate the parts. I have to say that he first time I encountered etched parts, I spent a lot of time trying to make the perfect cut, by separating and removing the holding tags, completely in one go. I now find that it is better to remove the part and trim the tags afterwards, my favourite tool for this being nail clippers. They crop the edge rather than scissor it and thus avoid distortion. The very design of the tool also enables a clear view of the area being cut so that there is a better chance of getting things right first time.

CHAPTER TWELVE

Guns

The guns were the core feature of design for the sailing man-of-war. How many and what size, basically decided the size of the ship and, in consequence, sail area and the number of hads that would be required. In fact, virtually everything to do with the making and sailing of the vessel came back to the armament specification. The ships were, in essence, sailing gun platforms.

The portrayal of the carriage gun, carronade, swivel gun and mortar in construction kits varies enormously from the fairly sophisticated to the downright crude. The design of the carriage itself varied according to period and the size of the gun it was to support. Many kits even fail to acknowledge the difference between the solid bed type and the truck and axle carriage. When it comes to the mounting of carronades, I know of one kit that uses a standard solid bed carriage without wheels! On the other hand, one British manufacturer provides properly researched guns and carriages, where a single carriage gun unit may comprise over twenty separate parts.

There is not much to go wrong when making guns, but there are one or two things that can make life a lot easier and make for a better job.

Brass gun barrels can look very smart, but it

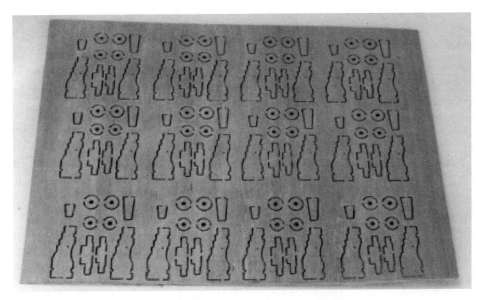

Fig. 12.1 Router cut gun carriage parts.

Fig. 12.2 Two sizes of assembled barrels and carriages.

is well to remember that after the mid-seventeenth century, most guns were made from iron, thus, the barrels would need to be painted. Don't forget the bore of the barrel.

Barrels were attached to the carriage top by means of capped trunnions, the latter being simulated in the kit by a suitably sized piece of

Fig. 12.3 Gun carriage rigging.

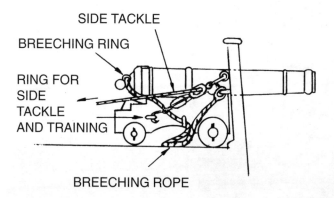

brass wire or rod that passes through the barrel. The ends of the trunnions need to be flat and not have that pinched and squeezed look left over from cutting the wire with side cutters. It is wise to check whether or not the barrels provided in the kit have the holes for the trunnions correctly drilled below centre. Most do not, but if they do, make sure that the barrels are mounted the right way up.

If the kit provides separate caps to fit on top of the carriage sides and over the trunnions, they are likely, these days, to be etched brass parts with a hole at each end.

They first need to be shaped in the middle so as to properly sit down onto the top edge of the carriage, after which they can be glued in place with thick cyanoacrylate. When this has set, holes are drilled to accept two shortened pins to represent the bolt heads. Carriage parts are pictured in **Fig.12.1**

The trucks, or wheels, on the carriages were of two different diameters, the larger at the front of the carriage and the smaller at the back, this difference being to accommodate the deck camber. The chances are, that when you come to mount the gun on the deck, you will find that it rocks. By drawing the carriage assembly over a sheet of abrasive paper laid flat on the bench, you will not only get rid of the rock, but provide four very small flats on the wheels that will improve the gluing area. Carriage guns of two different sizes are shown in **Fig.12.2**

The rigging of guns is not something that is seen on too many kit models. Most model makers seem to be happy with the compromise of fitting only the breeching rope, a heavy rope that restrained the gun carriage under recoil. To fully rig each gun, with gun and train tackle, would involve a further six rigging blocks and hooks and the smallest available tend to look oversize even at 1/64 scale.

The breech rope is probably best fitted by attaching the middle of the rope to the cascable

Fig. 12.4 The carronade.

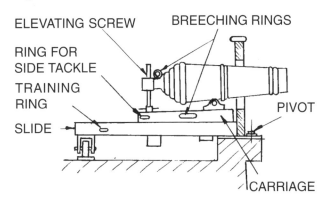

of the barrel first before lashing the ends to rings fitted each side of the gun-port. Remember that if the gun is *run out*, the breech rope will hang slack and will be taut only if the gun is in the *run in* position. A run out unit is shown in **Fig.12.3.**

Carriages used on English men-of war were

Fig. 12.5 The swivel guns on *H.M.S. Mars.*

frequently painted dark red and this should be recognised before actually mounting the barrel. *H.M.S. Victory* had its carriages painted with yellow ochre but I suspect that this was unique to that particular vessel.

The carronade was mounted on a sliding bed rather than a truck and axle carriage. The "fixed" part of the bed rotated laterally on a front-mounted pin, either inside or outside the hull, and the barrel was either trunnion or lug mounted to the sliding part of the bed depending on the period concerned. In all cases, carronades were rigged with a tackle system similar to that of a carriage gun and again most modellers seem content to rig only the breeching rope, **Fig.12**.

Do not get the carriage gun barrels mixed up with the carronades; they were completely different in appearance.

Finally, there were the swivel guns usually mounted on the bulwark rail. These may be found in the kit as castings, sometimes with a cast-in mounting spigot that merely requires a drilled hole for fixing or, in some later kits, a cast barrel supplemented by an etched brass cradle and pin. Such mounted swivels can be seen in **Fig.12.5**.

Period Ship Kit Models in Colour

Portsmouth 1796
695mm length
from a Mamoli kit.

Above: *Royal Caroline 1749*
830mm length
from a Panart kit.
Right: *The Pride of Baltimore 1988*
812mm length
from a Model Slipways kit.

Above left: *San Felipe* length 960mm from a Panart kit.
Above right: *H.M.S. Cruiser*, length 850mm from a Caldercraft kit.
Left: *H.M.S. Unicorn 1747* length 840mm from a Corel kit.

H.M.S. Royal William 1719
length 1143mm
from a Euromodel kit

Left: *Toulonnaise* , length 655mm from an Artesania Latina kit..Above: *H.M.S. Bellona 1760*, length 770mm from a Corel kit.

Armed Pinnace *1800*
length 620mm
from a Panart kit.

CHAPTER THIRTEEN

Ships Boats

English naval vessels carried a number of boats of different designs according to the rating of the vessel and as defined by Admiralty Establishments. However, there were often legitimate deviations from the rules and, if your kit doesn't have boats that are in strict accordance with the Boat Establishment of the day, it is not necessarily wrong.

Whatever numbers and designs you are faced with, one thing is for sure, the construction of model boats at the scales normally encountered, is one of the more challenging aspects of kit construction. In some kits, the problem has been got around by the provision of cast shells that merely require to be fitted out with wooden floors and thwarts. Others provide preformed composition or even plastic boat hulls to be similarly fitted out. However, these are frequently "standard" items and are not necessarily accurate for the model being made. Having said that, they are usually fairly simple to make and will pass muster to the uneducated eye. There is not too much in the way of further constructive comment to make about these items.

The real problems come with the small framed and planked boats that are intended to represent those designs, specified by the Establishments, for a particular vessel and it is

to the construction of these that this chapter is aimed. The method of construction is basically the same as for the ship's hull; a framework of false keel, floor and bulkheads that is then double planked.

Tools and Equipment.

The physical dimensions prohibit the use of pins and PVA for general fixing purposes; standard grade of cyanoacrylate being the best adhesive. PVA can, however, be used as a strengthening agent at various stages of the construction.

A cutting mat, together with a steel rule, and scalpels plus a few spare blades are needed to handle the cutting department. Swann Morton No's. 25, 25A, 26 and 27, held in 4-inch handles are a reasonable choice. A set of small files and fine abrasive papers are required for shaping and finishing, and a selection of small crocodile clips for some essential holding.

Making the Basic Framework

In most instances, the pieces concerned are presented as either laser - cut, or routed in sheets of fairly thin ply, the false keel and bulkheads being slotted in order to construct cross-halving joints. Do ensure that all parts are correctly identified before removing them from the sheet.

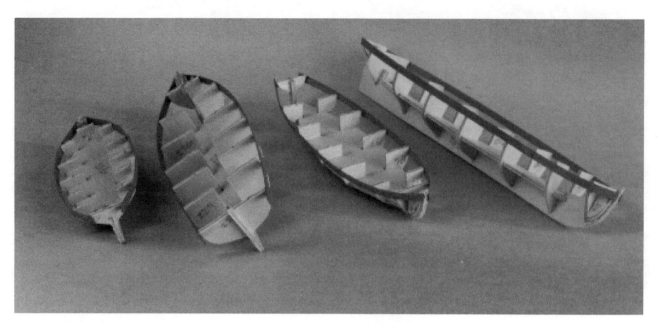

Fig. 13.1 Four boat carcases for *H.M.S. Agamemnon* with first planks in place.

The procedure for fitting the pieces together is to first attain the right fit of the joints; a light finger push fit is about as good a description that I can offer. Anything heavier than that will either distort or even break the assembly. Similarly, the floor is usually slotted to accept the ears on the top of each bulkhead. The preparation of the bulkhead edges must be left until after the framework has been assembled since the parts are really too small to be worked on individually. Dry assemble all parts to make a final check that bulkheads are in the correct sequence and that everything is straight and without distortion. The carcase can then be brushed all over with diluted PVA, or taken apart and reassembled using cyanoacrylate.

Irrespective of procedures outlined in the kit manual, I have always found it useful to strengthen the carcase by introducing small blocks between the bulkheads to sit in the longitudinal corners formed by the false keel and the underside of the floor. I make these blocks from scrap material with as large a section as possible, but without them protruding outside the lines of the bulkheads.

Having made the framework as strong as possible, the edges of the bulkheads can now be worked on with a lesser degree of concern about breakage. Scalpels and files are used to shape the outside of the framework so that, as with the main hull, the planking has the maximum possible seating area across each bulkhead edge.

In some kits, the edges of the false keel are left square so that a strip of material to simulate the prow and keel can be added later. Indeed, the instruction sequence may advise adding the strip before planking. If you haven't built too many small boats before, my advice would be to use the edges of the false keel as an aid to planking, sand a narrow flat on to the bottom and prow after planking, then add the strip last.

Therefore, when shaping the edges of the bulkheads, carry that shaping across to the centre of the false keel thickness at the prow and along the bottom. If the boat has a similar shape at the stern rather than a flat transom, do the same thing there as well.

Planking.

The first thing to remember is that the portion above the floor of all, or most, of the bulkheads has to be removed after planking. This means that the adhesive has to be used very sparingly on those relevant bulkhead edges, in

Fig. 13.2 The boats finish planked with upper parts of bulkheads removed.

fact, if the boat shape is kind to you, the top plank can be clipped and glued at each end with no adhesive at all on the intermediate bulkheads. For best efficiency, do not use old adhesive; it is false economy for this particular application.

The timber used for planking small boats is invariably only 0,5mm thick and probably only 3mm wide so it is wise to exercise control over applying the adhesive if planks are to be stuck in the right place and not to the fingers. Cock-

Fig. 13.3 The boats fitted out and painted.

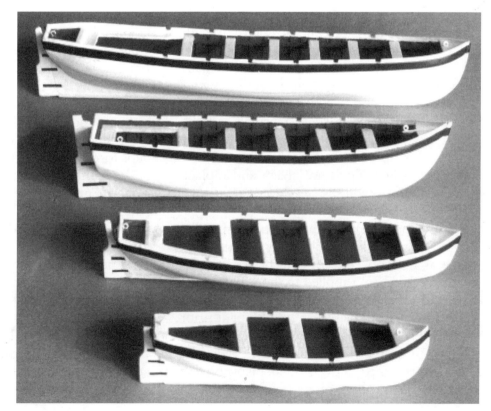

Fig. 13.4 The boats mounted amidships on *H.M.S. Agamemnon*.

tail sticks or toothpicks are ideal for transferring cyanoacrylate from a small pool in a glazed dish to the work-piece. The nozzle of the adhesive container is definitely out!

The nature of the planking material normally provided in kits suggests that it will cut better when wet and to this end it is worth keeping half a dozen strips in soak. I usually cut the length needed from each in turn, returning the shortened strip immediately to the water. Make sure that your scalpels are sharp and replace blades as soon as you suspect the edge has gone off.

As mentioned above, the first plank, parallel and cut over-length, can normally be glued into place at the top edge of the boat with the cyanoacrylate being applied to those bulkheads fore and aft that do not have to be removed later, **Fig.13.)**. All planks should be bent prior to assembly using a nipper or thumb and fingers. Having fitted the first plank on one side, the ends are trimmed and a similar plank on the opposite side is put in place. If it is possible to

clip the plank tightly to the tops of the intermediate bulkheads, this is a bonus worth taking advantage of. The second plank each side will have to be tapered, the degree of tapering being established in the same manner as used on the hull. Again the plank should be clipped at each end if possible, but this time the top edge should be glued to the plank above.

Should it not be possible to use crocodile clips fore and aft, then the plank should be glued at the front end first and held in place with the fingers until set. The plank can then be pulled round the frame to be glued at the back end. Glue can be applied along the plank edges afterwards.

When the planking reaches the line of the floor then, of course, the planks may be glued to the edges of all bulkheads. Planking should be done alternately, side to side, each being trimmed fore and aft before putting on the next plank. When all planks are in place, it strengthens the shell considerably to brush it over on the outside with dilute PVA and leave overnight to harden before rubbing down.

The second planking is easier since adhesive can be applied to the whole surface but it is important to shape the planks as neatly as possible so as not to leave unsightly gaps. It is helpful, of course, if the boat shell is ultimately to be painted, but tidier work is essential if the finish is to be in natural wood.

Now comes the time to remove the top parts of the bulkheads, **Fig.13.2**, line the floor with slats and put in the ribs. Slats and ribs normally require planking strips reduced on width, sometimes down as small as 1,5mm or 2mm, with the resultant fiddly application of adhesive. The top edges of the shell should now be trimmed to shape.

An inner rail to support the thwarts is then added, followed by the thwarts themselves, taking care to fit the ends neatly against the inside of the shell.

Although not always specified in the kit instructions, I always feel that a neater result is attained if the top edge of the shell is capped. This may be done with card or plasticard and the method used is to make the capping in two parts, port and starboard. Draw round the outside edge of the shell, carefully cut to this line with scalpel or scissors, then draw a parallel line inside the cut edge to represent the inner line of the capping. This can be delicate work, best done with a scalpel using minimum force.

A narrow flat may now be filed to form seating for the aforementioned stem, keel and rudderpost. Thole pins, or rowlocks together with a rudder and tiller are then added prior to painting and finishing, **Fig.13.3**.

Oars were sometimes kept in the boats but could be stowed perhaps for security reasons as a deterrent to desertion should the vessel happen to be anchored offshore.

Depending on scale, oars may be required to be fabricated from wood, usually small dowel material, with flat strip for the blades. In some kits, they may be presented as etched brass parts which obviously saves some time in construction, although many consider them to look "not quite right," having a somewhat flat appearance. Even so, coaxing a bend into the actual blade part can enhance their appearance.

Boats may have been hung on davits astern but frequently were mounted on beams, gallows or spars amidships as shown in **Fig.13.4**

CHAPTER FOURTEEN

Masts and Bowsprit

It is amazing that there are still some people around who think that once you have made the hull and put all the fittings on, that's the model nearly finished; maybe that is because there are so many museum models to be seen without masts and rigging. In truth, of course, there is still a lot to do. Indeed there are some model makers who will tell you that the best is yet to come, and that the hull is merely a base on which to demonstrate the artistry of masting and rigging!

Certainly, there are some simple masts comprising a simple, tapered pole upon which is hoisted a spar and sail. However, on larger

Fig. 14.1 A home-made rod support.

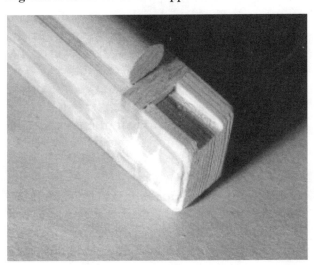

vessels where three, or even four, masts have to support a vast sail area, the design of the mast becomes very complex and one that evolved over centuries of sailing experience. The model maker will become aware of these complexities as progress is made towards the building of the larger 17th - 19th century sailing warships.

There are several processes that the kit builder will need to master in order to make masts. Tapering and squaring are the two most significant.

Tools Required

A David plane and a miniature spokeshave are used for removing the bulk of material when tapering. A good half-round file or Perma Grit abrasive tools are next in the sequence to be used followed by a selection of abrasive papers for finishing. A miniature electric drill, craft knives and a razor saw will also be needed. White PVA and cyanoacrylate will be required to stick things together. A home-made rod support is something easily made and, although not essential, certainly makes the tapering job less hazardous.

My rod support was made by taking a 300mm length of 30 x 20mm timber and cutting a slot 3mm wide x 3mm deep down its entire length then fixing a stop at one end. This permits most sizes of dowel to rest snugly along the slot with the stop at the end taking the thrust of planing.

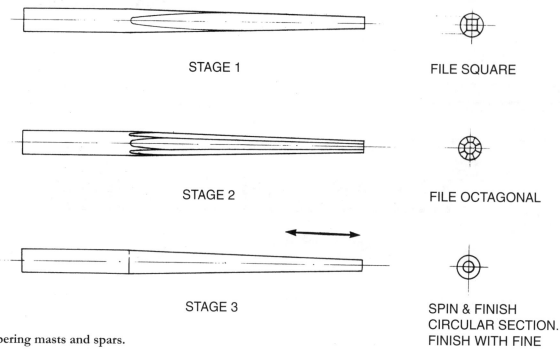

STAGE 1

FILE SQUARE

STAGE 2

FILE OCTAGONAL

STAGE 3

SPIN & FINISH
CIRCULAR SECTION.
FINISH WITH FINE
ABRASIVE PAPER

Fig. 7.2 Tapering masts and spars.

I have a 5mm slot on the opposite face to handle larger diameters of dowel rod, **Fig.14.1**. This device can be used in the vice or even held down on the bench by hand.

Tapering

This technique is based on the assumption that the modeller does not have a lathe available and has to rely on his handwork to produce the goods.

Most households have a DIY quality electric drill, or the more ambitious modeller may have a 12 volt mini-lathe, either of which can enhance the finishing process.

Check that the kit has provided enough dowel rod of the appropriate size to permit the required length to be cut off with an additional 25mm. This provides for a "holding" piece at the bottom and a "tidying up" piece at the top, the use of these becoming apparent as the making of the mast proceeds. Should the kit not allow you to find this extra length it merely means that additional care will be needed so as not to damage the ends. The overall length cut off should, of course, include that section at the top, or head, of the

mast that may require squaring later on.

Along the length of the mast make a pencil mark to indicate where the required taper starts. This may be at deck level, or in some cases a certain distance above deck level. On the top end of the mast, use a compass or circle gauge to draw a circle indicating the diameter at the small end of the taper.

The dowel is then laid into the aforementioned home-made support and a flat planed from nothing at the start of the taper to one tangential to the circle drawn on the end of the rod. The dowel is then rotated through 180 degrees and a similar flat planed on the opposite side. Appropriate rotations will enable eight flats to be planed thus finishing with an octagonal section at the top end of the dowel rod. Should it be found that on one side of the dowel, the wood tends to tear, then discard the plane and use a file for that particular flat or flats.

For those who wish to be more precise in achieving the octagonal shape, the dimension from the first flat to the diameter opposite is R + r where "R" is half the diameter of the dowel rod and "r" is half the diameter at the small

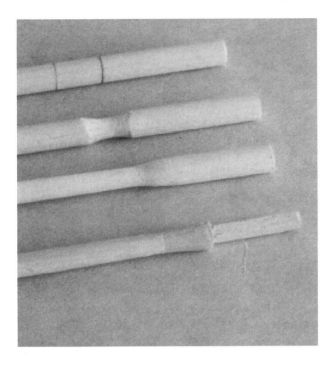

Fig. 14.3 Producing a topmast with integral hounds.

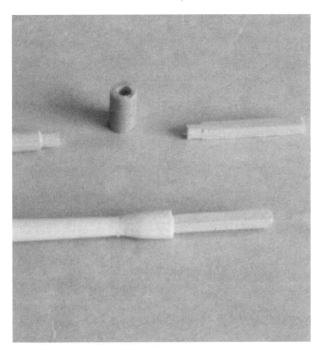

Fig. 14.4 Producing a topmast with separate hounds.

end of the taper being produced. Having rotated the dowel to do the flat on the opposite side, then the size across the flats is 2r. With experience, many modellers will produce the octagon by eye without even the guidance of the circle drawn on the end of the rod.

However, this does take a bit of practice and is probably not recommended for the less experienced.

The eight corners should now be removed, either with the plane, or the file, so that the octagon is converted to a circle. The large end of the rod may now be placed into an electric drill or mini-lathe and spun for finishing with abrasive papers. The final finishing should be done out of the drill or lathe by sanding lengthways by hand up and down the taper. If the dowel had previous been cut to finished length, then take care not to over-tighten the chuck and mark the work-piece. Refer to **Fig.14.2**.

This is where the advantage of the extra length comes into play. The chuck on the lathe or drill may have marked the dowel rod at the large end and, at the other end the abrasive paper will almost certainly have rounded off the very end of the taper. The latter can be removed by

sawing off about 5mm with a razor saw and, when cut to finished length the chuck marks at the other end will be cut off.

A complication to the tapering process arises where topmasts, or topgallant masts, have hounds. These are the swellings or projections just below the masthead and which support trestletrees and crosstrees. These obviously prevent the through passage of a plane and therefore dictate the use of an alternative method. I have no doubt that most experienced modellers will have their own pet procedure for dealing with hounds, but the best method is always that which you have personally developed, to suit the tools available, and the way in which you like to work.

One way is to file a half-round shape all round the masthead at a point just below the position of the hounds, so that the diameter at the root of the shape is basically the diameter at the small end of the taper. It perhaps needs a little bit of practice to ensure that the shape is kept concentric with the outside diameter of the dowel. If you have a mini-lathe this is an ideal job for it. I then use a miniature spokeshave, pulling the tool toward me from the bottom

Fig. 14.5 Lower mast showing combined bibs and hounds supporting trestletrees.

Fig. 14.6 Lower mast on *H.M.S. Agamemnon* showing side cheeks bound by wooldings and iron hoops.

end of the mast up into the half-round shape, to produce the series of flats to form the octagonal section, **Fig.14.3**. The shape of the hounds proper may then be developed, using either scalpel or file, or both. When shaping the hounds, take note whether that part of the mast immediately above them has a square or round section and act accordingly.

Alternatively, produce the taper on the mast as if the hounds were not there, then taking a piece of larger diameter dowel, drill a hole axially through a length equal to that of the hounds and of a size to suit the small end of the taper. This may then be glued onto the mast and its final shape be developed *in situ*, **Fig.14.4**.

Squaring

The top end, or head of the mast, may need to be square in section. This is normally done by filing, the sectional size being determined either by a quoted dimension on the drawing, or by having to scale off. The art is to keep the surface being produced, flat and straight. The first flat is fairly straightforward and may be filed to almost finished position. The mast is then rotated through 180 degrees and the second flat produced, again to almost finished size, but

keeping it *absolutely parallel* to the first. The third and fourth flats are similarly produced. The results can be seen in **Fig.14.0**.

A square or octagonal section may also be required at the heel of the mast. A word of warning is in order at this stage because, in many cases, the size measured across the flats of the section at the heel is nominally the same size as the diameter of the mast immediately above. Strictly speaking, this means that you have to start with a dowel diameter that is the size of the square or octagon when measured across the corners, rather than the flats. Unfortunately, many kits do not provide a large enough size of dowel to do this, but there is a way out. File a square section onto the heel of the mast then, using scrap material, build up the size of the square to the required dimensions, or trim and file to an octagonal section as required.

Mast Parts

Some of the items listed below feature in several places on the mast and spar structure of a sailing vessel and I make no apology for repeating them, where necessary, to bring continuity to the section under discussion.

Bibs. On most kit-built models the bibs on

Fig. 14.8 A bowsprit with jib boom, cap and dolphin striker.

lower masts are an integral part of the hounds and are those projections forward of the lower mast that provide added support to the trestletrees, crosstrees and top, **(Fig.14.5)**.

Cheeks. These are pieces of timber fixed to either side of the lower mast, their length from the underside of the trestletrees down being dependant on the period of the vessel in question, **Fig.14.6.**

A flat is required to be filed onto each side of the mast in order that the cheeks seat properly. These flats are usually done at the same time as

Fig. 14.7 Sequence of tying wooldings.

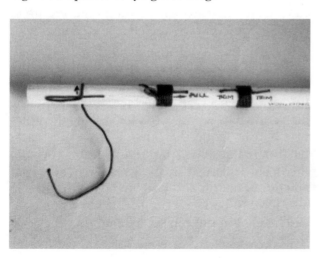

the squaring of the masthead to ensure that they are in the same plane.

Front Fish. A strip of timber fixed to the fore face of a mast, either as a strengthening piece, or to prevent the chafing of the bottom edge of the sail on masts fitted with iron hoops. A flat is required on the model mast for the front fish to sit correctly.

In the latter part of the eighteenth century the front fish was known as a rubbing paunch.

Iron Bands. These gradually superseded wooldings towards the end of the eighteenth century. When fitted to masts, they passed *under* the faces of side cheeks and *under* the front fish or rubbing paunch and were positioned between the iron hoops on the lower mast.

These are easily simulated by strips of black cartridge paper cut to a width appropriate to the scale of the model and stuck onto the mast with PVA. Black cartridge paper is provided in some kits for this purpose. If your kit is not one of those, then a spare page from a photograph album will do the trick. It is important to cut the strips all the same width since the iron hoops on a mast are sufficiently close together to make any variation of width very noticeable.

For best effect, overlap the joint, cut through both layers and remove the surplus to make a neat butt joint. However, wait for a few minutes until the glue has started to go off as the initial drying causes the paper to shrink and leave a gap at the joint.

Iron Hoops. These should not be confused with iron bands and were fitted around the mast and the masthead, usually on the foremast and mainmast only, of sailing warships and were basically to bind the various mast elements together. They passed *over* the cheeks and *under* the front fish or rubbing paunch, if fitted, **Fig.14.6.**

They are made and applied in the same way as the iron bands above.

Mast Battens. These are frequently omitted from kit-built models unless a fairly large scale is being used. They are vertical strips of timber, two of which are fixed to each of the faces of the masthead adjacent to their vertical edges.

They are there to prevent rigging from chafing the masthead, thus will fit *over* the simulated iron hoops.

Wooldings. These were rope bindings around the lower masts and sometimes the bowsprit to give added strength. Depending upon the size of the vessel in question, the number of these fitted onto the mast varied. Fitting them to models is a matter of careful measurement in order to ensure equal spacing and of applying the same number of turns of thread at each position, **Fig.14.6**.

The method of application involves laying a thread loop longitudinally along the mast then winding on the required number of turns over the loop. When the requisite number has been put on, the free end is passed through the exposed end of the loop and pulled under the binding. The wooldings are then brushed with dilute PVA and the ends trimmed, **Fig.14.7**.

One aspect of these features rarely found on the kit-built model is the wooden hoop that was nailed to the mast at the top and bottom of each of the wooldings. For many modellers, the making and fitting of wooden hoops would not be a practical option. However, one model that caught my eye in this respect, was where the model maker had neatly put on the wooldings in black thread and had then added one turn, top and bottom, of a slightly larger tan thread. It did indeed make a significant difference to the appearance of the mast and I needed to look quite closely to see exactly what had been done. Certainly an award of "ten out of ten" for innovation was deserved, but alas, the model has to be of fairly small scale, or the twist in the tan thread becomes too evident and gives the game away.

Making the Bowsprit

The Bowsprit. This varied in design considerably, earlier vessels carrying a sprit top and topmast at their forward end and later ships having a jib boom, **Fig.14.8**. There were examples of vessels carrying a combination of all three.

Cut off an over-length piece of dowel taking

into consideration technique outlined above and remember to include the length required at the head to fit the bowsprit mast cap, and the length required for fixing inside the fore part of the hull, if relevant.

Taper the bowsprit using the octagon/circle technique with plane or file noting that there may be two tapers, one running forward towards the cap and the other running towards the butt end. Having got this basic piece made, check that the area of the hull into which it fits is properly sized and shaped and adjust if necessary, ensuring that the angle at which the bowsprit sits relative to the waterline is correct.

We now come to an awkward bit, the fitting of the sprit topmast knee or, if the model is of a vessel with a jib boom, the bowsprit cap. The knee will probably be a pre-cut part if the kit is of more recent production, and the two adjacent faces will be at their correct angles. The longer side of the knee, which sits on top of the bowsprit, has the same angle of inclination as the bowsprit. The shorter side should be perpendicular to the waterline so that the sprit topmast, when in place, is upright.

The Bowsprit Cap is shown in **Fig.14.8**. If the bowsprit is to be furnished with a jib boom however, the problem is usually more of a nuisance because too many kits provide you with a bowsprit cap that has two holes drilled through *square* to the faces! Unfortunately, these holes serve no useful purpose whatsoever and, unless the holes are very small in diameter, it is better to make a new cap from scratch so that the holes can be drilled through at the angle required. Drilling holes onto an angled face is fraught with problems and, if you are making a new cap from scratch, it is better to consider starting with a large enough block, drill the required holes through square from one face, then shape the block down to cap size. In fact, drilling the holes first before sizing the outside faces is a better bet for making any parts with holes through them, particularly if the holes are anywhere near an edge. The top and bottom edges of the cap also have to be faced off to the same angle.

Having got the cap sorted out, the spigot on the fore end of the bowsprit has to be formed.

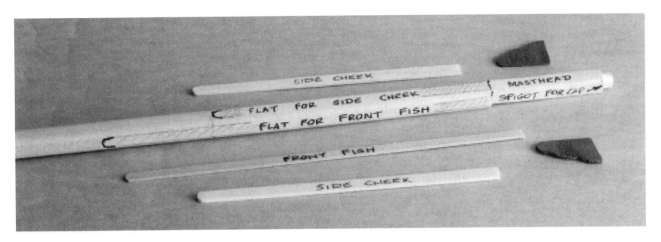

Fig. 14.9 Filing flats on masts for masthead, side cheeks and front fish.

It should be concentric with the bowsprit, long enough to pass completely through the cap, but with its rear stop face vertical when the bowsprit is at its proper angle to the waterline. The cap should not be glued to the bowsprit at this time.

Bees. These were two small platforms that sat port and starboard on the sides of the bowsprit just aft of the cap. The shape of their outer edges depended on the period concerned and, to be absolutely correct, the outer edges should be slightly raised so that the two bees are not level with each other. Two holes will be required in each to take later running rigging.

Iron Bands or Wooldings. These should be applied in their correct positions and, if relevant, also things like the jib boom saddle, the fairlead saddle and gammoning cleats. The

first two of these are frequently supplied as pre-cut parts, but in any case, are not difficult pieces to make. Cleats, on the other hand, can be a bit of a problem for the less experienced and the following method for making them is recommended.

Cleats. From the strip of timber specified, cut off a length at least 50% longer than the finished cleat using a *sharp* scalpel or craft knife. I emphasise *sharp*, because at the usual size of strip provided, the grain is often coarse and open and the piece must be *cut* off and not *pushed* off. Cyanoacrylate is probably best for sticking the cleat in place and if a thin film is spread onto a glazed surface, the over-length cleat, when picked up with a pair of tweezers, can be dabbed onto the film then stuck into place. The

Fig. 14.10 Ironwork.

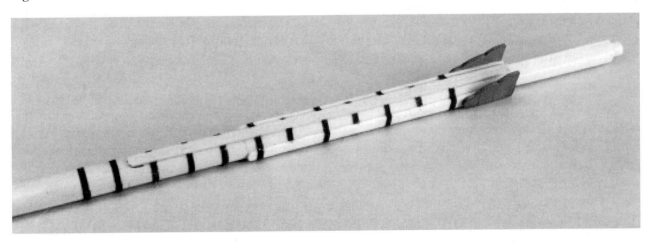

advantage of it being over-long is that the positioning at the time of gluing only has to be accurate in one plane. Its position longitudinally, and its finished length can be attained by using the scalpel once the glue has set. This is particularly helpful in the case of gammoning cleats, where their position on the bowsprit has to follow a vertical line to prevent the gammon lashing to the prow from slipping down the bowsprit. The backs of the cleats may now also be tapered as required.

This process can be adopted for all cleats used in mast and spar making, remembering that it is important to make a flat seating for them.

In the case of gammoning cleats, it is helpful to dry assemble the bowsprit to the hull and eyeball the vertical run of the gammon lashing so that the cleats can line up with its rear edge.

The Jib Boom

This is an extension to the bowsprit passing through the cap to the jib boom saddle where it is usually lashed to the bowsprit, (Fig.14.8). The boom has one taper, a rigging stop at its outer end and a hole to represent a sheave just behind the stop or neck. In some instances the jib boom may be further extended by a flying jib boom, which would be heeled into the bowsprit cap to run alongside or orientated at 45 degrees to the jib boom. Its position at the outer end of the jib boom would be held by the flying jib boom iron or, in some cases, a small two-holed cap.

Dolphin Striker

This is a spar, usually of rectangular section affixed in a downward attitude to the front face of the bowsprit cap, (Fig.14.08). In its original form, introduced at the very end of the eighteenth century, it supported the martingale stay and merely had a notch in the end. It gradually evolved into a more complex spar which to handle several other stays as well. In fact, U.S.S. Constitution sported a double dolphin striker in the form of an inverted vee to support even more stays and guys.

It is frequently best to fit this after assembling the bowsprit to the hull since it then becomes easier to make sure that it has its correct attitude. Consider a pinned and glued joint to be the preferred manner of fixing.

Collars

Collars seized with closed hearts and/or deadeyes should be attached to the bowsprit in the appropriate places for the later rigging of shrouds, bobstays, forestays, etc. These attachments should be very secure and I normally employ multiple, overhand knots prior to brushing with adhesive. However, if working on a larger scale model, the collars may be fashioned and attached in the proper manner.

Making the Lower Masts

The ongoing notes are equally applicable in whole or in part to all the lower masts, so I have not written a separate section for each. The main and fore masts are usually the same in construction although differing in dimensions. The mizzen is usually simpler in that it doesn't have any ironwork and may not have side cheeks.

Lower Mast

Cut off an over-length piece of dowel taking into consideration technique outlined above and remember to include the length required at the masthead to fit the mast cap, and the length required below deck.

A check should be made to ensure that the dowel drops smoothly into the hole in the deck and that it then stands upright when viewed from the front or back of the model and assumes the correct rake angle when looked at from the sides.

The procedure is then to mark the start of the taper required and using a plane or file, produce the octagon section at the small end then, further reduce to a round section as described in the section on tapering, above.

The second stage is to square section the masthead portion and form the spigot to fix the mast cap. If your kit has pre-cut parts to make the trestletrees and crosstrees, it is quite a good idea to dry assemble these parts at this stage and use them as a gauge to size the squaring of the masthead and to get the

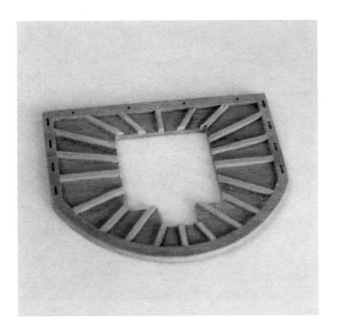

Fig. 14.11 The upper surface of a top fitted with battens.

Fig. 14.12 A typical 16th century round top.

orientation of the cheeks and front fish correct. The flats on the sides of the mast to seat the cheeks should be filed in the same plane as the square on the masthead. The flat on the front to seat any rubbing paunch or fish is filed at 90 degrees to the cheek seating, **Fig.14.9**.

Cheeks and Front Fish. The cheeks and fish should then be made and the seating and general fit checked for correct orientation. These items are normally fabricated from strip material but there is a growing tendency in the marketplace to provide them in kits as preformed parts.

Do *not* glue them in place yet.

Check the drawings and instruction manual at this stage to see if the mast needs to be painted before adding any ironwork or wooldings.

Ironwork. The positions of iron hoops and iron bands should now be marked, the strips of black cartridge paper cut to width and glued to the mast as described above **Fig. 14.10**. The bands should be fitted first and the glue left to thoroughly dry; the band should be carefully removed from across the seating faces for the cheeks, before gluing the cheeks in place. Do not, at this juncture, fit hoops around the

masthead it may interfere with the assembly of the trestletrees, crosstrees and top.

The hoops are now fixed in position over the cheeks and, in a similar manner to that used for the bands, should be cut away from the seating face for the front fish, which may then be glued in position.

Wooldings appear on models of ships of an earlier period, they are tied over both cheeks and front fish and should be applied as described in the notes above, **Fig.14.7**.

Do remember that while these notes indicate the three types of mast binding, the usual combination would be either wooldings, or hoops and bands. Such bindings were rarely used on the mizzenmast.

Hounds and Bib. The integral hounds and bibs should now be considered. These are normally just stuck on to the upper faces of the cheeks to add further support to the trestletrees. However, the angle that their top edge takes up relative to the mast is most important and, to understand the fundamental issue, it has to be realised that the surface of the top and the framework upon which it sits has to be parallel to the waterline, *not* at 90 degrees to the centreline of the mast. So, by putting the mast into the hull and again using the dry assembled

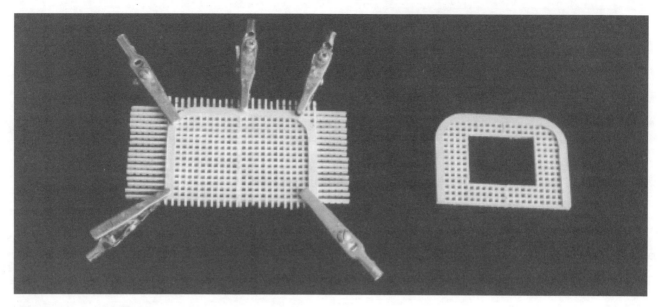

Fig. 14.13 A top with gratings for *H.M.A.V. Bounty*.

trestletrees with their longer top surfaces as a gauge, the correct angle for setting the hounds/ bibs can be better achieved. Alternatively, the hounds can be added after fixing the trestletrees, crosstrees and top assembly in place.

Tops

I have found that in most kits, making this top assembly as a separate mini-project pays considerable dividends. By first gluing the trestletrees and crosstrees to the underside of the top platform, as well as stabilising the platform, it is easier to get all relative positions right and simpler to hold for drilling holes and fitting eyebolts. In some cases the upper surface of the top platform will have a rim and the actual edge may be required to be capped, the latter being done after notches for the deadeye strops to the topmast, and the futtock shrouds, have been cut in. In some cases, pre-cut lots may have been provided.

The shape and complexity of construction varied according to the period. On vessels up to around 1700, tops were circular and had angled sides, **Fig.14.12**, which were often planked with a capping rail around the top edge, the supports for the sides usually being an integral part of the battens radially spaced around the floor of the top. A good kit will provide these parts pre-cut, but care is still needed to get the spacing correct. The fixing of the top rail is particularly important since it is through these that the deadeye strops for the topmast shrouds will pass. The angular sides of the top providing clearance for attaching the futtock shrouds below.

Later vessels had tops with straight backs and sides although the basic principles of design remained. Again, there will be a number of battens to arrange in a set pattern on the upper surface of the top. Getting the pattern symmetrical calls for careful measurement and accurate trimming of the ends of the wood strip being used. It is best to start with the central or lateral battens and use a pair of dividers to determine the position of the others. The corners of the lubber holes in the platform proper are useful gauging points for getting the inner ends of the battens in the right place, **Fig.14.11**.

Another variation arises in the case of some merchant vessels where the top may be a framed grating. These are constructed in a similar fashion to deck gratings but without the battens described above, **Fig.14.13**.

There will probably be a number of eyebolts to insert on the rear upper surface of the top, plus several on the underside of the crosstrees. Reference to the relevant rigging drawing will ensure that these are put in the right place.

Further reference to the rigging drawings may also reveal the later application of crowsfeet, which should indicate that a number of holes around the front edge of the top would be necessary. These should be drilled before assembling the top to the mast, noting that there is always an even number and thus, *not* one drilled on the front centre of the rim.

If at all possible, I like to fit the lower deadeyes for the topmast shrouds to the top platform at this stage or, in the case of models of earlier period vessels, to the rim of the round top. Some kits provide etched brass strops for this purpose, but on many smaller scale models the deadeye is rigged with thread, the tail of which then passes down through the top to become the futtock shroud, **Fig.14.13**. In this case it is important to ensure that the thread is well secured into the hole in the top since it is disastrous if the deadeye joint becomes loose while attaching the lanyards to the topmast shrouds.

The top assembly may then be glued in place on top of the hounds, again checking that it sits parallel to the waterline when the mast is stepped. Do not glue the mast cap onto the spigot on the masthead at this stage, but the masthead iron hoops may now be put in place. The futtock shrouds may be left hanging down until later. *See Chapter Eighteen - Futtock Shrouds.*
Bolsters. These were strips of timber, quadrant shaped, and fitted to the top surface of the trestletrees to protect the lower shrouds from the sharp edges of the structure.

You can normally expect to form the section yourself using a suitable piece of square sectioned strip. **Fig.14.14** shows bolsters mounted on topmast trestletrees, but those for the lower mast were basically the same.

A final look over the lower mast assembly will identify any missing eyebolts prior to doing any further painting that may be specified. This may involve painting the doublings, i.e. that area between the bottoms of the hounds to the mast

cap, with matt black paint. Alternatively, this painting may be left until the whole mast assembly has been achieved.

Making the Topmasts

The tapering and squaring should be done as outlined above, not forgetting to take into account the hounds at the top end, and the possible octagonal or square section at the heel. Make sure that the square section at the masthead is in the same orientation as the section at the heel. One or more holes drilled through the mast fore and aft may be required for the running rigging and are best put in before assembly.

Trestletrees and Crosstrees. Again see **Fig.14.14**. Whereas those for the lower masts were essentially supports for the tops, when fitted to the topmasts and topgallant masts, they were basically spreaders for the associated upper shrouds. According to the rake angle of the relevant masts, sometimes the ends of the crosstrees were bent back to correctly position the lower end of the shrouds. The higher quality kit will provide pre-cut parts, thus obviating the need for the modeller to put the bend in.

If this is something that has to be undertaken, I have found that it is far better to cut the shape into a sufficiently wide strip or piece of ply rather than try to bend a strip of the correct section. My reason for this advice is that the

Fig. 14.14 An upper crosstree assembly - note bolsters.

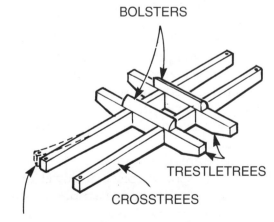

CHECK WHETHER CROSSTREES CURVED
BACK, OR WERE STRAIGHT

ends of the crosstrees are not restrained in any way and, having been bent with heat and wetness they will, in time, and with any changes in the display environment, tend to straighten! Holes at the outer ends of the crosstrees should be drilled before assembly to the trestletrees. Cross-halving joints are the usual method of bringing these features together.

The upper trestletrees and crosstrees should be checked for correct fit at the masthead but *not* glued in place at this time.

The cap that fits on the lower masthead should be slipped over the top of the topmast and down onto its spigot, at the same time locating the heel of the topmast into the front part of the lower trestletrees. Assuming that the correct alignments can be attained, that the lower masthead and bottom end of the topmast are parallel, and no adjustments are required, the upper trestletrees and crosstrees may now be glued in place. The position for the fid hole may now be assessed and drilled laterally through the heel.

Fid. This was an iron or wooden stop bar, which fitted athwartships through the heels of the topmast and topgallant masts and stopped the masts on the upper edges of the trestletrees. Not all kits show them, but they are an easy addition to make and will enhance the model to advantage if exhibiting or competing.

Making the Topgallant Masts and Royals

A similar procedure to that for the topmasts should be employed, the exception being that there will be no trestletrees and crosstrees to consider. What can prove to be a little difficult is the making of the topgallant and royal masts as one integral piece. The diameters involved are that much smaller and not so easy to get concentric without some sort of turning facility. However, there is a way out and one that might be considered to be preferable to turning.

If you adopt the principle of making the hounds as a separate piece of dowel, drilled to sit on the top of the mast prior to shaping, then the hounds can locate on only half length, leaving the upper half to accept the royal mast.

The royal mast did have a slight taper and

was fitted with a truck at the top end, which should be fitted before assembly to the topgallant mast hounds.

Final Mast Assembly

The bringing together of the three sub-assemblies, **Fig.14.15**, described above requires attention to strict alignment in the vertical plane and parallelism at the doublings when viewed on the side. Your model may have only two sub-assemblies or it could have four in some cases, but the requirements remain the same in terms of relative alignments. Most of the features concerning mast parts and their assembly are shown in **Fig.14.16**. It is also important to note assembly sequences; masthead caps for the lower masts frequently need to be fitted loose onto upper masts before assembling tops. A dry run is usually the best way to establish an appropriate assembly sequence.

Finishing. If any painting required has not been done earlier in the sub-assembly stage, now is the time to get the paint-pot out. Check the requirements for your particular model; not all vessels had painted masts, some had painted lower masts only, with black at the doublings and natural wooden upper masts, and some were left natural throughout. There are modellers who abhor paint in any shape or form and leave the entire model to exhibit the beauties of the natural wood, whether painting is specified or not.

Rigging Blocks

The drawings should be carefully studied to identify all the various types and numbers of rigging blocks that fit directly onto the mast assemblies. It is strongly recommended that these be put in place before stepping the masts to the hull. See *Chapter Nineteen for details of tying blocks*. It is also wise to ensure that holes in blocks are completely clear before tying them in place. Even the smallest whisker at the entrance to, or exit from, the hole can be a problem later on when rigging. Murphy's Law dictates that such a block will always be in a place that is the most inaccessible. Having been caught out in the past,

I always run a drill through *all* blocks at the outset.

Provision for Fixing the Yards

Although I personally do not advocate fitting the yards to the masts before stepping the masts to the hull, provision for the fixing needs to be made at this juncture. This is merely the drilling of a hole, 1mm diameter, in the front face of the mast to accept a brass wire peg of similar diameter mounted in the back of each yard. Try to avoid drilling the hole completely through both mast and yard. However, before drilling such holes, the decision to fit sails or not has to be made. If you are not, then the yards will be down onto the caps. If you are going to rig up a set of sails, then the yards will be hoisted to their uppermost position on the masts.

Once the masts have been put up, every on-going operation contributes to decreasing the amount of space available for the hands to work on the model and so anything that can be conveniently done beforehand should be.

CHAPTER FIFTEEN

Yards and Spars

Many of the techniques involved in making yards and spars are basically the same as those used for making the masts. However, it is also true to say that the properly made yard is not necessarily the simple task that first appearances would lead you to believe.

Vessels prior to the end of the seventeenth century are most likely to have yards that were entirely of round section. Ships from later periods will have a mixture of yards with a totally round section and yards with an octagonal centre section, the latter being largely confined to the lower and topmast yards.

Tools

The tools required for making yards and spars are the same as those used for making the masts.

Tapering

For round-sectioned spars, the method adopted is exactly the same as for the masts described above. The procedure is similar and differs only in that the operation becomes twofold, from the middle of the yard out to either end, again see **Fig.14.2**.

Yards with an octagonal centre section require a slightly different technique and the first consideration has to be given to material size. Some manufacturers still overlook the fact that, for such a yard, the diameter of the basic dowel has to reflect the size of the octagon measured across the corners, and not the largest diameter of the yard, or the size of the octagon when measured across the flats.

In these circumstances, the kit builder has three options; make the yard slightly undersize, build up the centre section with battens, or purchase a length of larger diameter dowel.

The first is undoubtedly the way most people will deal with the problem since, at the scales normally involved, the error will be small enough to be unnoticeable to all except the really knowledgeable.

Building up the centre section with battens is, in some specific cases, the correct approach since this was the actual construction for larger yards that were scarfed together in two pieces.

The final option, using larger dowel, will involve more work to reduce the new dowel size to the required octagonal shape. Bearing in mind that the corner size of the octagon will be less than the dowel diameter, the production of the octagonal section requires a much greater degree of accurate measurement, rather than being able to eyeball and use the diameter of the dowel as a sighting reference.

For the purposes of this chapter, I have assumed that the manufacturer has got things right or, if not, the modeller is going to adopt the first and approximate option quoted above.

As in the case of tapering masts, it will ultimately be useful to cut the dowel over-length with about 3mm extra each end. Using the aforementioned rod support, next produce the octagon section *parallel and throughout the length of the yard*. The required length of the centre portion (usually about 25% of the total length) is then marked onto the piece and the octagon tapered from those marks to the end of the yard and finally the edges taken off to form a circular section. The ends are cut to finished length and rounded off.

Yard Arm Cleats. These should be made in the same manner as the gammoning cleats described in the section about the bowsprit. These were fitted in pairs, one to the fore and the other to the aft side of the yard arm, **Fig.15.1**. Their length, and distance in from the end should be established with a scalpel after the adhesive used has thoroughly set. It is important to make flat seatings on each yard arm for the cleats, such flats being in the same plane as two of the opposite flats of the octagonal section.

Sling Cleats. Fitted to the fore side of lower yards and level with the yardarm cleats mentioned above, these may be provided as pre-

cut parts on larger models, but more usually have to be fabricated from strip material. I find it better to make these up directly onto the face of the yard and again tidy up the shape with a scalpel after the glue has dried, **Fig.15.1**.

Stop Cleats. These are found on the centre fore face of the upper yards and indeed on lower yards of later period vessels. In a similar way to other cleats, if cut over-length and glued into place on flats filed on the front face of the yard, they can be trimmed to shape and length after the glue has dried, **Fig.15.1**.

Iron Hoops. If the yard had been made in two parts, as was the case with some larger vessels, and battens used to strengthen the scarf joint and thus form the central octagonal shape, they would have been bound together with a series of iron hoops. The drawings should indicate the number required for the model in hand. They can be simulated with strips of black cartridge paper.

Stunsail Boom Irons. These devices allowed the stunsail booms to be slid out from the ends of the yards to set the stunsails. There were two at each end of the yard, one usually mounted in the end of the yard and one set some distance along the yard to support the inner end of the boom. They should be set at 45 degrees between the top and fore faces of the yard, **Fig.15.2**.

These outer irons sometimes have to be made from wire, bent to shape by the model maker and fitted into a drilled hole in the end of the yard. Some trial and error work will be required to attain the right height of the boom above the yardarm surface.

Should the kit provide a cast ring for the main part of the iron, its attitude will still need to be the subject of some care and attention.

The inner irons may also be cast parts but are not a source of trouble in their assembly. If the outer irons are made from wire, it is often the case that the inner irons are represented by bands made from strips of cartridge paper. To make the outer iron, the wire is bent around a piece of dowel of stunsail boom size to form a ring and then bent to provide a shank like a large eyebolt. A right-angled bend is then put into the shank to make the spigot that fits into

Fig. 15.1 Cleats.

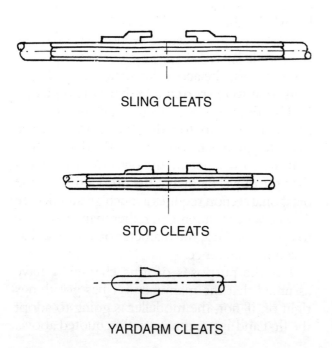

SLING CLEATS

STOP CLEATS

YARDARM CLEATS

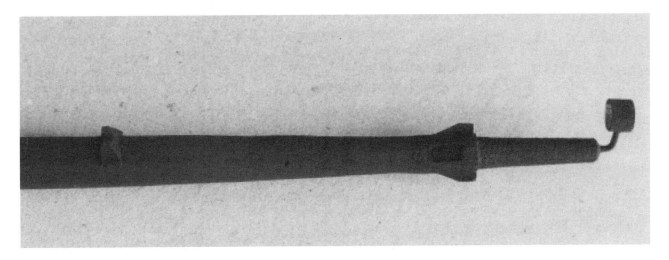

Fig. 15.2 Stuns'l boom irons.

the end of the yard. It is establishing the distance from the ring to this bend that needs the care to ensure that the boom is basically parallel to the yard.

Holes. Sheaves were in evidence at the ends of some yards and these are represented by drilled holes; these must definitely be drilled before putting the yards on the mast.

It is undoubtedly advantageous to provide a hidden fixing of the yards to the masts by means of a brass pin. I use 1mm diameter wire fitted centrally into the rear face of the yard and a similar size hole in the appropriate place on the front of the mast.

I do not normally fit the yards to the mast until I am actually ready to do the rigging.

Stirrups. These are nearly always made from wire and frequently take the form of long shank eyebolts. This is really cheating, due to the fact that stirrups made from thread just do not hang right. Some kits advise a simple insertion into a drilled hole in the bottom of the yard. Others show them wrapped around the yard and hanging down from the rear of the yard, the latter being the more accurate representation. Whichever method you use, the important thing is to get them all hanging to the same depth below the yard. I normally form the eye in the end of the wire before cutting the stirrup to length, bending the wire around the shank of a suitable size drill. Getting the eye neatly formed is difficult enough without having to get it in the

right place as well. A piece of card cut to size is used as a gauge to ensure that the eyes are in their correct position below the yard.

Painting. Yards may be required painting and this should be done before adding the footropes and rigging blocks.

Footropes. The main problem with footropes is getting them to look as if they are hanging correctly under their own weight. This is not and easy task and requires considerable patience. However, there are two things that can be of help; try not to twist the thread as you lash it onto the yard and pass it through the stirrups and give it a brush with dilute PVA before fitting. Don't wait for it to dry before using it then, having got it tied on, stroke it into the sagging curve required as the glue begins to go off.

Rigging Blocks. Like the masts, yards are furnished with a number of blocks of varying styles and sizes including the brace pendants. These should be put on before assembling the yards to the masts. See Chapter Nineteen for details of tying blocks.

A full set of yards and spars with stirrups footropes and blocks can be seen in **Fig.15.03**.

The Mizzen Yard

Like other yards, this had two tapers but, in this instance, the lengths of the tapers were not necessarily equal, the bottom half being shorter than the top. Sling cleats were fitted in the same

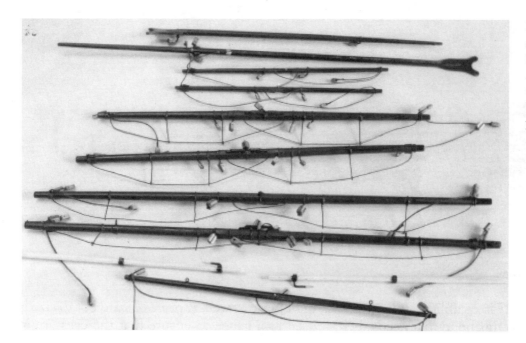

Fig. 15.3 Set of yards, spars and stuns'l booms for *H.M.S. Mars*. Note stirrups and footropes applied before assembly of yards to masts.

manner as for other yards at the conjunction of the two tapers. It was lateen rigged that is, set at an angle fore and aft onto the lower mizzenmast.

Boom and Gaffs. These are the spars that largely replaced the mizzen yard by the end of the eighteenth century. The boom was the lower, and longer, of these two spars with jaws at the butt end, which nestled around the mizzen and secured with single parrels or a truss. It normally had one taper throughout its length.

The upper and shorter spar was the gaff, which was constructed in the same manner as the boom. In some rigging configurations, both spars featured whereas in others only the gaff was used.

The jaws are frequently pre-cut parts that have to be fitted to the butt end of the spars. The easiest method of attachment is to cut a long vee in the tail of the jaws and fashion a taper onto the butt end of the spars to fit. Alterna-

tively, a parallel slot can be cut into the end of the spar to match the thickness of the material from which the jaws are made. This is a much more hazardous operation especially when working with small diameter spars.

It is generally found easiest to tie one end of the parrels or truss to the jaws before trying to assemble the spars to the mizzen.

It is worth checking the drawings or manual to see whether these spars should be painted. If so, this is another task that should be done before assembly.

Stunsail Booms. These were spars that extended the effective length of the yards in order to carry additional sails.

These are best made in conjunction with the boom irons and should be fitted to their relevant yards before assembly to the masts. They have one taper and, on kit models, seldom exhibit any of the essential extending tackle a fact which gives scope to the more enterprising kit builder.

CHAPTER SIXTEEN

Sails

The manufacture of sails for static model ships is a subject that sometimes seems to fall well outside the normal model making skills and more within the realm of the expert needle-worker. The main problem that besets the modeller is the quality of the material. For the kit builder, who largely has to work with what he is given, the difficulties can be of added significance to a point where a major decision has to be made; whether to rig the model with sails or leave them off!

I will say right from the start that I am one of those modellers who do not like sails on a static model of a period ship unless it is a waterline model or part of a diorama. However, when doing an in-depth review of a kit that includes sails as part of the package, I feel that I should at least look into the practicalities concerned. I therefore came up with a policy that I considered a fair assessment of the situation and one that anybody can justify applying to a kit built model. I take into account the nature of the material provided in the kit and assess whether or not it will ever make a reasonable looking sail. I look at the needlework content and its complexity and balance the need against my limited abilities, asking myself if I can make a reasonable job of it without spoiling an otherwise nice model. If I come up with a

negative answer to either of those key questions, then I take the easy way out and rig the model without sails.

However, I recognise that not all modellers will share my feelings on the matter, so I will endeavour to highlight some of the problems and the methods that I adopt to get round them.

Material quality varies enormously. Some cloths fray, it seems, by merely looking at them. Most require some sort of dyeing process to make them look anything like real canvas, and none of them are likely to "hang" right, the finished sail resembling a limp and damp string vest on Monday's washing line. If you really wish to put sails on the model, and are prepared to buy some material to replace what has been provided in the kit, then I would suggest you consider ecru, or unbleached linen, and see if its weave and general quality is suitable for the model in hand. Stay away from the man made fibres. Silk has the best hanging qualities due to its greater *weight to area* ratio but it is almost impossible to permanently get rid of the sheen.

Scale is an important factor in assessing the needlework content. A large-scale model requires more complex needlework. Seams have to be simulated by parallel rows of stitches and in many cases, the fitting of boltropes can prove a nightmare.

Colouring the cloth brings to light all sorts of ideas, from the use of proper fabric dyes to the tinting of the material with cold tea or coffee. I have tried the latter and it works reasonably well and is worth a try, rather than getting involved in the messy business of using formal fabric dyes. It depends on how much colour is desired as to how many times the coffee is applied, or indeed, how strong it is made. Like many things in model shipbuilding, it all comes down to trial and error and personal taste; so you will forgive me if I don't recommend a particular brand of coffee, just make sure that it is black.

Most, if not all, materials will require pressing before any further work can be contemplated, particularly if the cloth has been through the dyeing process. A fairly low setting suitable for rayon is usually adequate used in conjunction with a damp cloth. Do not apply the iron directly to the cloth; any dressing in the material will stick to the sole of the iron.

Fig. 16.1 The sails on *Leida* are stiffened with matt clear varnish and have drawn seams.

Fig. 16.2 Spiral lacing of a square sail to a yard.

The sails can then be marked out, a process that is necessary for any needlework anyway, but also as an alternative to stitching if the model is small enough, say below 1/72 scale. For marking out, I use a flat lead propelling pencil with 0,5mm thick leads in order to maintain a constant thickness, and an HB grade for a reasonable density of line. All seams and hems are drawn including any reef bands. The sail is then sprayed with matt varnish; not only does this provide a degree of stiffness for the later shaping of the sail, but also imparts some translucency so that the seams and bands can then be drawn in their correct position on the opposite side of the sail. It further seals the weave of the cloth and thus obviates fraying when the sail is finally cut from the sheet.

The sheet is then pinned down with a drawing pin at each corner of the sail and the thread representing the boltrope pulled tightly around the pins. The thread passes totally round each pin to form cringles at the corners of the sail. The boltrope and the edges of the sail are then brushed with dilute PVA. When it is seen that the thread is securely stuck down, the sail is cut from the sheet, cutting as close as possible to the outside of the boltrope.

On larger scale models and especially those with sails rigged, the edges of the sails will be required to have cringles. These are small loops to which running rigging such as buntlines, brails and bowline bridles will be attached.

Blocks are then added as necessary and the completed sails put to one side until required for rigging.

I will not presume to write anything about stitching sails; I am neither competent nor qualified to do so. Knowing my limitations, I either use the method described above or do not fit sails to my model at all. However, as **Fig.16.1** shows, the method works well for the right model.

At what stage sails are attached to the yards is largely a matter for personal choice. For reasons of accessibility for hand and fingers when rigging, I normally fit them to the yards before fitting the yards to the mast, this being left until the standing rigging is basically complete.

For square sails, staysails and jib sails, I use separate lashings appropriately spaced along the head of the sail. For spankers and drivers, a continuous length of thread, spirally lacing the relevant edges of the sail to the gaff and mizzen. Spiral lacing is also sometimes used for the square sails of smaller vessels as shown in the accompanying photographs **Fig.16.1** and **16.2**.

When considering the spanker, it helps to rig both boom and gaff to the sail before fitting the spars to the mast in order to get them at the correct angles before rigging. This is far easier than getting the spars in place, only to find that the sail has been made to a slightly different set of angles and thus has a very unnatural hang to it.

CHAPTER SEVENTEEN

General Rigging Notes

The myths that surround the rigging of model boats cause many people to be put off ever starting a period ship model and, although it is true to say that the fully rigged ship is something of a mind boggling sight, when you consider that it is largely a matter of quantity rather than complexity, the rigging becomes a much less daunting task.

The rigging can be considered to be in two parts; the standing rigging, usually in black thread, that in basic terms holds all the masts in place, and the running rigging, usually in tan or natural thread, that is used to set the yards in their correct attitude and adjust the set of the sails.

Items of standing rigging are illustrated in **Fig.17.1** and **Fig.17.2**. Note that the crowsfeet shown in the latter diagram should not be confused with the crowsfeet to the mast tops, described later.

The kit will include a set of rigging drawings, which provide a visual guide to where each line starts, through which blocks they are threaded, and an indication as to which direction they finally go towards the deck. This latter point should have a number attached to it that relates to the same number on the belaying plan, which is where it is tied off. That takes care of the running rigging.

The drawings should also provide you with information as to where and how the standing rigging is attached and by what means it is kept under tension.

Each line is put up separately and so rigging just boils down to exercising a lot of care and patience. I have seen beautiful models made by first-timers with no maritime knowledge whatsoever, in fact, the man in my introductory story still wasn't really sure about port and starboard when he had finished his *Royal Caroline*. Having said that, some knowledge of what each part of the rigging does, is undoubtedly a great advantage to the model maker, but such wisdom usually comes with experience.

So, apart from the care and patience, where do the difficulties lie? Undoubtedly, one of the biggest problems is doing things in the right order. It is very difficult to lay down rigid rules because the sequence can vary considerably according to the type of vessel being rigged. However, there are one or two things that can be said that may prove to be of help.

Read the instruction manual and study the drawings. In most cases these will reflect the correct procedures decided during the building of the prototype, either by specific notes in the manual, or inferred by the sequential numbering of the drawings. If such instruction has not been given, then I recommend using the very generalised procedure outlined below.

1. Standing rigging - black thread
bowsprit and all masts.
Lower shrouds.
Upper shrouds.
Futtock shrouds.
Ratlines.
Stays.
Apply any remaining standing rigging, apart from backstays, which should be left until the end of the rigging process.

2. Fit the yards (and sails if relevant).
Trusses and parrels.
Jeers, slings and ties.

3. Running rigging – natural thread – start basically with those lines that belay at deck-level centreline and work upwards and outwards to provide the best accessibility at all times. Obviously, this procedure can vary enormously depending on the type of vessel being consid-

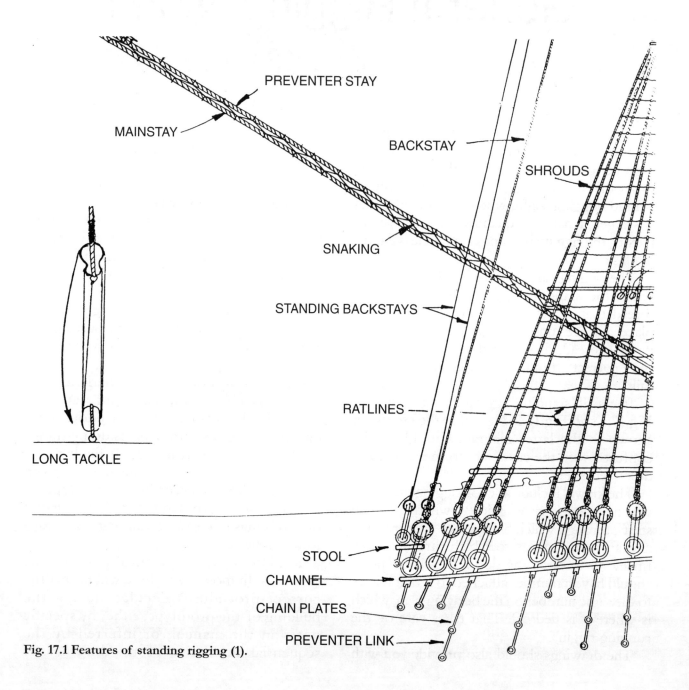

Fig. 17.1 Features of standing rigging (1).

Fig. 17.2 Features of standing rigging (2).

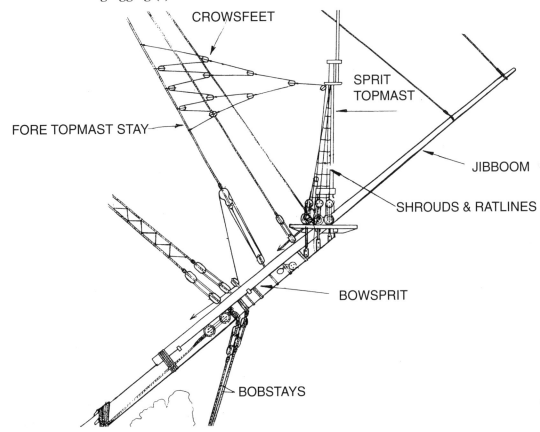

CROWSFEET

SPRIT
TOPMAST

FORE TOPMAST STAY

JIBBOOM

SHROUDS & RATLINES

BOWSPRIT

BOBSTAYS

Adhesives

Much has been said about the pros and cons of the various adhesives available to the modeller and their application to the rigging process. In the end, like so many other things, the choice becomes one of individual preference. However, there are some advantages and a few disadvantages attached to most of them, and perhaps the best solution is to be selective and choose the correct or most convenient for the job in hand.

Without doubt, the recommended adhesive for most rigging applications is dilute PVA, the main proviso being that it should be used to seal an already soundly tied lashing, seizing or knot, and thus permit very close trimming of ends. Obviously, the latter operation being performed only after the glue has dried.

Cyanoacrylate is an adhesive that needs to be used with great care. It doesn't merely glue

the threads together; it can completely alter their physical structure, to the point where undue stressing of the thread can cause breakage. It can also cause discoloration, which is virtually impossible to get rid of, and thus results in a messy joint.

Knots, Seizings and Lashings

For larger scale models, the use of the correct lashings, knots and seizings are usually shown on the kit drawings. These provide the best approach, inasmuch as they provide a sound mechanical fixing and the use of adhesive simply seals the ends of the thread for trimming purposes. For some of the smaller scales, however where, perhaps, rope-work can take on a grossly oversize appearance, some degree of technical adjustment, or cheating, has to be done. The theoretically correct method has to be substituted for a simple hitch that is more reliant on the adhesive for its success, for instance. In fact, most of my rigging is put up using half hitches, clove hitches or overhand knots or variations thereof. These are all then sealed with adhesive and trimmed closely with a scalpel, or, if the end to be cut off comes away from the knot at the right attitude, a pair of cuticle clippers. I prefer these to any other cutters and, if kept specifically for this purpose, they will last a lifetime.

This may seem like a stupid remark to make, but do ensure that when cutting off a length of thread for rigging, you allow sufficient to make any knots or other fixings. A typical case in point is the tying on of ratlines; you will be surprised how much length is required just for the hitches and the handling.

Finally, before picking up your tools, remember to take off any watches, rings or other jewellery and roll up your sleeves. Cuff buttons and any of the others are notorious for catching on any rigging that has already been put up, sometimes with disastrous results.

CHAPTER EIGHTEEN

Standing Rigging

Cordage

Except for things like lanyards and crowsfeet, the standing rigging is almost entirely put up with black thread to simulate tarred rope.

Unfortunately, the quality of thread provided in some kits is not as good as it might be in that it tends to be too hairy. This certainly does not look right on the finished model and, even worse, it becomes a prime target for dust adhesion, the bane of all ship models that are not cased or otherwise enclosed. In most cases the problem can be overcome by pulling the offending thread through fingers coated fairly liberally with PVA. This needs a little bit of practice so as not to entirely clog up the twist of the thread, but it does usually flatten down the hairiness. It can also have the effect of taking some of the twist out of the thread that may sometimes be a nuisance when rigging.

Bowsprit Rigging

Gammoning . This lashed the bowsprit to the stem of the ship, **(Fig.18.1)**. Depending upon the size of the vessel, there may be one or two sets of gammoning.

You need enough thread to make about ten turns of gammoning and about 20mm of the leading end of the thread stiffened with cyanoacrylate to form an integral bodkin. The other end is tied to the bowsprit immediately in front of the gammoning cleats and then led down through the head rails to the elongated hole in the stem. The thread is kept to the fore end of the hole before leading it back up and over the bowsprit immediately to the fore of the initial tie. When feeding down to the hole in the stem, the thread should be kept aft of the previous pass and when coming up over the top of the bowsprit, it should be kept forward of the previous pass. This gives the appearance of a twist in the gammoning.

The gammoning is framed between stem and bowsprit with the same number of turns as the gammoning itself.

Bobstays. One or two bobstays may be pertinent to the model in hand; both would be attached to a hole in the stem and, at the upper end be seized with a heart or deadeye. A lanyard connects the bobstays to hearts or deadeyes on collars below the bowsprit, **Fig. 18.1**.

I fit the hearts or deadeyes first, attach to the stem and then rig the lanyards to tension the bobstay.

Shrouds. These fit either side of the bowsprit, usually from deadeyes and lanyards at the bowsprit end, to hooks and eyes on the bows, **Fig.18.1**.

Tie on the hooks first and assess the position of the deadeye at the other end. Make two identical shrouds, hook in place and pull up with lanyards.

Martingale Stay. This is basically a line that ran from the end of the jib boom, through a

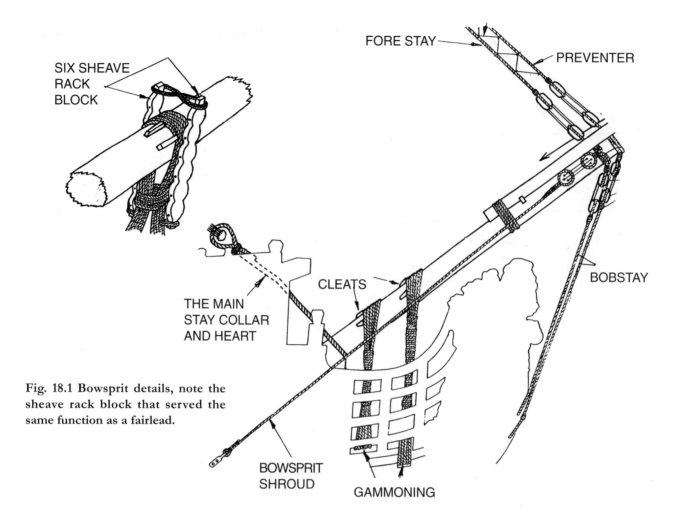

SIX SHEAVE RACK BLOCK

THE MAIN STAY COLLAR AND HEART

CLEATS

FORE STAY

PREVENTER

BOBSTAY

BOWSPRIT SHROUD

GAMMONING

Fig. 18.1 Bowsprit details, note the sheave rack block that served the same function as a fairlead.

hole in the end of the dolphin striker then up to the underside of the bowsprit, where it was attached with block and tackle. There were several variations of the martingale stay in practice, but the one I describe here that is integral with the martingale backstay, seems to be the one most commonly found in kit models, **Fig.18.2**.

The block on the bowsprit is one that should have been attached at the time of making the bowsprit assembly. Take the required length of thread and tie onto the specified block, noting that the thread for the tackle should be attached at this time. Take the free end through the dolphin striker from the rear side and, assessing the correct distance between the two blocks at the bowsprit end, attach the free end to the end of the jib boom before reeving the tackle and belaying at the point specified on the belaying diagram.

Lower Shrouds to the Masts

Shrouds were normally set up in shroud laid rope, that is, four strands laid right handed around a rope yarn core. However, three or four strands laid left handed to make a cable laid rope were also used for lower shrouds and stays. Kits do not differentiate between these types of rope, but the manner in which the lanyards are reeved through the deadeyes should correctly reflect the type of rope used, (see the section on lanyards below).

The lower shrouds are normally the first to be put up. They are rigged in pairs, the forward starboard pair followed by the forward port pair and so on moving aft down the channels that hold the lower deadeyes. I am sure that everyone will have their own pet way of doing shrouds and, it is true to say that my way is somewhat different to what it was twenty years ago. It has evolved by virtue of mistakes,

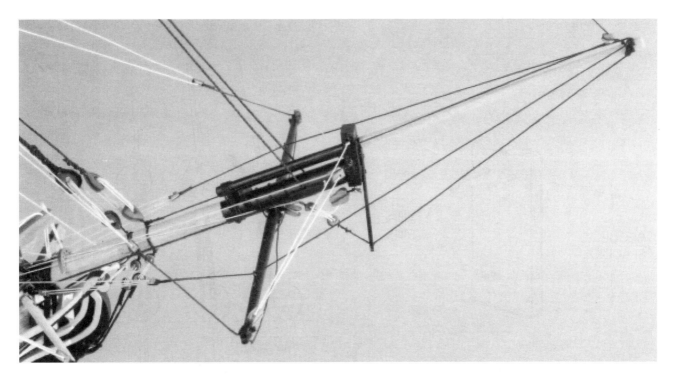

Fig. 18.2 Bowsprit rigging. Note the martingale stay and the fairlead at the bottom of the bowsprit.

convenience and slightly arthritic fingers.

I cut a suitable length of black thread and fit a deadeye to one end. To do this, I wrap the end of the thread around the deadeye, twist it once and nip it at the throat between thumb and forefinger, then with the other hand, take a

Fig. 18.3 The sequence of tying deadeyes to shrouds.

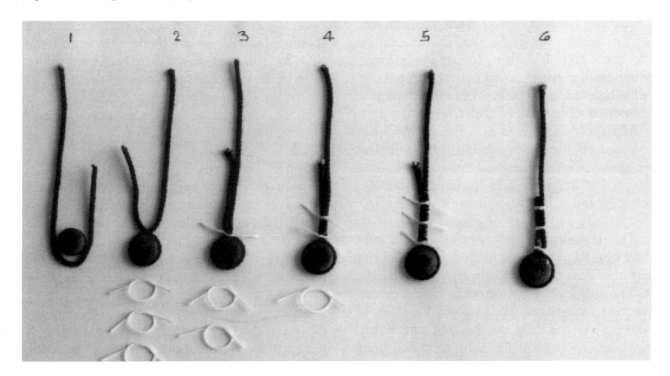

Fig. 18.4 Deadeye spacer.

Fig. 18.5 The sequence for rigging lanyards to shrouds.

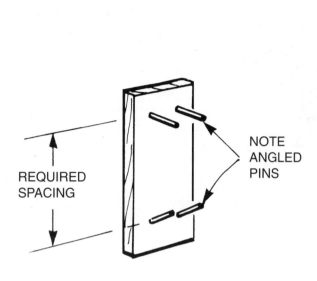

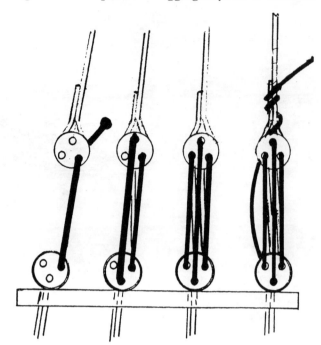

piece of finer thread previously formed with an open overhand knot, and slip it over the deadeye. The second finger of the hand holding the throat traps one end of the knot, while the other hand pulls the opposite end up tight to represent the throat seizing. A similar approach is then used for the middle and upper seizings, **Fig.18.03**. The whole fixing is then brushed with dilute cyanoacrylate taking care not to get any in the holes of the deadeye. Before putting this to one side to dry out, I check that the deadeye is in its correct orientation, i.e. one hole adjacent to the throat and in line with the shroud. Then I proceed to make an identical length for the port side by which time the seizings and other surplus ends on the first one are dry enough to be trimmed.

The sequence for fitting deadeyes to shrouds shown in **Fig.18.3**, uses natural thread for the seizings. This was done for purposes of clarity.

The deadeye is temporarily linked to the second deadeye from the front on the channel concerned, (this may be the first one if the modeller is left-handed), using a scratch built

separation gauge, **Fig.18.4**, or a temporarily reeved lanyard. The shroud is led around the rear of the lower masthead and back through the doublings and down towards the first deadeye on the channel. After readying another open overhand knot on the bench, I then fit a second deadeye in the same manner as the first, keeping the shroud reasonably taut so as to better judge the position of the deadeye as being the same as the first. The two shrouds are then tied together about 25mm below the level of the top to keep the deadeyes in their relative positions while fitting the lanyards. This tie is *not* glued.

Lanyards. These are rigged using natural thread. Because the lanyards were, during the life of the vessel, liable to require pulling up to tighten the shrouds, they were not tarred, but tallowed or greased to permit free running through the holes of the deadeyes.

While, kits do not consciously recognise, or provide, the correct twist of thread to properly represent the correctly laid rope for shrouds, it is important for the model maker to reeve the

Fig. 18.6 Lower deadeyes and lanyards.

lanyards in the proper manner. The kit drawings should indicate the correct passage of the lanyard through the deadeyes recognising the requirements for cable laid or shroud laid rope as applicable, the latter being the more usual and the one I use for the ongoing discussion, **Fig.18.5**.

I take a length of suitable diameter thread and put a stopper knot close to one end, seal and trim it. The first 10 - 12mm of the other end, I stiffen with cyanoacrylate to form a sort of bodkin and trim the tip diagonally. The bodkin end should not be any longer than 12mm or it causes difficulty when threading through the lower deadeye, (you can't get it out from the rear of the deadeye). I find that tweezers are an invaluable aid to threading and pulling through.

The end is threaded into the forward hole of the upper deadeye on the inboard side, pulled through to the stopper knot then down to the front hole of the lower deadeye, pushed through then up to the rear of the upper, central, hole of the top deadeye. This process continues until

the last hole, the left hand in the lower deadeye has been threaded from the front. The tension of the thread is taken up to pull the shroud reasonably taut. It is not tied off above the upper deadeye at this stage.

(For cable laid shrouds, the end of the lanyard is threaded into the aft hole of the upper deadeye on the inboard side, pulled through to the stopper knot, then down to the rear hole of the lower deadeye, pushed through and up to the rear of the upper central hole of the top deadeye. This process continues until the last hole, the right hand in the lower deadeye has been threaded from the front). I then treat the second pair of deadeyes in the same manner and, having left the ends of the lanyards unhitched, the level of the deadeyes may now be fine-tuned. Having satisfied myself that the balance is about right, I hitch the free ends of the lanyards around the shroud just above the upper deadeye.

The final tension in the first pair of shrouds is attained by pulling the tie applied at 25mm below the top, up the shrouds to sit as close as

Fig. 18.7 Futtock shrouds.

Fig. 18.8 A shroud cleat on the fore topmast. Note also the last of the crowsfeet.

possible to the masthead. Glue and trim.

The next shrouds to be rigged are the forward pair on the port side followed by the next pair on the starboard channel, and so on until all deadeyes on the channels of both sides have been set up, **Fig.18.6**.

Sheer poles. These were iron bars lashed to the outside of the lower shrouds just above the upper deadeyes on the lower shrouds to prevent the shrouds from twisting. They were more prevalent on vessels after the end of the eighteenth century when shrouds were more usually set up with cable laid rope. On most kit models they are made of wire and are lashed to each shroud.

Futtock Stave. In a similar fashion to the sheer pole, they were lashed across the outer face of the shrouds, just down from the underside of the tops. The rigging drawing in the kit should indicate the actual dimension or have a scale drawing that can be measured. Wire would be the usual choice of material and, once fitted, the futtock shrouds can be rigged.

Catharpins. These were lines rigged between the port and starboard futtock staves to keep the shrouds from being pulled out of line by the futtock shrouds. There were a number of ways in which catharpins were fitted and if a kit recognises their use, then the rigging drawings should adequately indicate their correct passage to and fro across the vessel.

Futtock Shrouds. Referring back to *Chapter Fourteen*, when making the tops, the deadeye strops for the topmast shrouds were rigged with thread and the free ends left hanging down below the top. These now become the futtock shrouds and pass once around the futtock stave and are then seized to the shroud below the stave. Great care should be taken not to put too much tension on the futtock shrouds so that the shrouds are pulled out of alignment, particularly important if catharpins are not rigged.

Larger and more detailed models where the deadeye strops for the topmast shrouds are pre-formed, either as wire parts or cut from an etched brass sheet, will have a portion protruding below the underside of the top and have a hole through it. In these cases the futtock

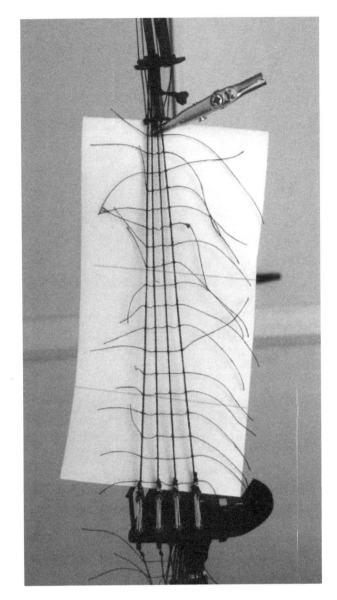

Fig. 18.9 The use of a background when rigging ratlines.

shroud will either be seized to the hole or be fitted with a hook to the hole. The lower end of the futtock shroud will then be rigged to the stave and seized to the lower shrouds as described above, **Fig.18.7**.

Shroud Cleats. It is probably better to add the shroud cleats (if any) at this stage. They normally fit to the inside of the shrouds just above the level of the deadeyes or sheer pole. Use cyanoacrylate as the initial means of fixing then supplement this with two seizings. Cast cleats are usually notched at the point of seizing which makes the job a lot less fiddly. A shroud cleat

Fig. 18.10 Take the line across the front of the next shroud and feed to the back.

can be seen attached to the inner side of the foremost starboard shroud deadeye in **Fig.18.8**.

Topmast Shrouds

The manner of fitting the topmast shrouds is the same as that for rigging the lower ones as described earlier in terms of sequence and with deadeyes and lanyards at their lower end. However, they will probably not be rigged with sheer poles, although may be fitted with futtock staves to secure the bottom ends of the topgallant shrouds. Catharpins are not applicable.

Futtock Staves. These will normally be made from wire, again seized in position just below the trestletrees/crosstrees. As before, the stave should be seized to all shrouds.

Topgallant Shrouds

These are set up in the same sequence as other shrouds but not usually with deadeyes and lanyards. Instead, the shrouds pass down from just above the hounds on the topgallant mast to holes in the outer ends of the cross-tress and thence to the futtock stave on the topmast shrouds, where they are seized to the shrouds

in the way already described.

Ratlines

This stage of the rigging operation is without doubt the most tedious and time-consuming part of the project, the tedium coming, for the most part, from the shear amount to be rigged and the associated number of knots to be tied. Before making suggestions as to how to actually rig them to the shrouds, there are a few things to bear in mind. Don't try to do the whole lot in one go; rig perhaps one flight at a time, and in between rig a couple of the stays before going back to the next flight.

Tools required

A scalpel, fine nosed tweezers, small side cutters or cuticle clippers and dilute PVA with brush will be needed.

Spacing

It would seem that ratlines were set between 13 and 15 inches apart, obviously taking into account the energy required for a sailor to quickly get from deck to top, and then do whatever his job demanded. I normally choose

Fig. 18.11 Pull the line forward, through the loop and tighten.

to use 15 inch spacing, not because I believe it to be the more correct end on the range, but simply because it results in less ratlines to rig.

To keep some consistency in the spacing, I cut a strip of card or 0.5mm plasticard to a width equal to the spacing required and of a length that will cover the widest span of shrouds. Due to the angle at which the shrouds are inclined, the spacer will sit comfortably on the ratline previously rigged and permit the knots on the current ratline to be eased into position on the shroud using a pair of tweezers.

Cordage. The quality of the thread can make a great difference to how it "hangs" on the shrouds. Black thread seems to be the first choice of most manufacturers for ratlines, but in some cases the dyeing process adds a stiffness that is not conducive to getting the ratlines to look right. Tan thread of the same size often ties, and takes the knot better, although this advantage is offset by the fact that after all the ratlines have been tied on, they have to be brushed over *in situ* with Indian ink. Overall, the amount of time spent is not too much different whichever path is followed; just remember to thoroughly protect the deck and

fittings from any possible splatter if the ink method is specified.

Application. If you are right handed, work from left to right and *vice versa* if left-handed.

Before starting to actually tie on the ratlines, a sheet of white or buff coloured paper propped between mast and shrouds affords a better background against which to work. Ratlines are inevitably a strain on the eyes, particularly if you are rigging in black, and the plain backdrop greatly assists maintaining focus, **Fig.18.9**.

Cut off a suitable length of thread to rig the first ratline. A reasonable guide is to measure across the widest span of the shrouds and double the result, taking note of the actual dimension.

Pass one end behind the left-hand shroud, bring it forward between the first two ratlines and form an overhand knot. Pull it tight on the first shroud so that the short end of the thread is to the left and the long end to the right. The short end left for trimming should measure about 15mm. With practice, I found that the use of tweezers to manipulate the thread around the shrouds and to make the knot was less cumbersome than using fingers and thumbs.

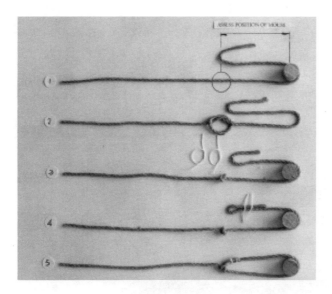

Fig. 18.12 Making a mouse and eye.

Tweezers further help to avoid twisting the thread, which is something that should be avoided if you want the ratline to hang correctly.

Pass the long end across the front of the second shroud, back between the second and third then forward between second and first. Tie another overhand knot on the second shroud. When pulling the knot up tight, if the thumb and forefinger are squeezed together between the first pair of shrouds, finger at the back and thumb at the front, it will help hold the shroud separation and prevent the shrouds being pulled out of line. It is very important to keep the shrouds straight at all times and not impart that "pulled in" appearance.

Tying ratlines to the fifth shroud is shown in **Figs.18.10** and **18.11**.

Proceed across the span of shrouds in the manner described in the last two paragraphs and cut off the surplus thread leaving 15mm for later trimming. Measure the length of the surplus just removed and deduct that from the overall length noted earlier. The result will give you the length to cut for the next, and subsequent, ratlines and which will provide a minimum of 15mm overhand at each end for trimming. This procedure should ensure that you don't have too much wastage and run out of material before you have finished.

Fig. 8.13 The rigging of closed hearts. Note the closer view of the fairlead on the bowsprit.

Fig. 18.14 Snaking the stays and the crowsfeet rigging.

I normally tie on four or five ratlines at a time by eye, erring on the wide side then, using the spacer mentioned above, adjust the second ratline to the first by laying the spacer on the first and, with tweezers, gently ease the knots of the second down the shrouds until they sit on top of the spacer. The remaining ratlines are adjusted in sequence in the same way. All the knots on the first batch of ratlines are then brushed with dilute PVA before tying on the second batch.

When all the ratlines on one flight of shrouds have been done and the glue allowed to thoroughly dry overnight, I trim the ends close with the clippers.

Topmasts and Topgallant Mast Backstays

These are rigged in the same way as the shrouds, sometime to the same channels but also at times to separate stools on the hull fitted with deadeyes and chain-plates. Depending on the size and style of the model I frequently find that these are best left until almost last in the rigging process since they can obstruct free access to hands and fingers getting towards the centre of the model during the ongoing rigging and belaying.

Mizzen Stay

Starting from the mizzen top with a mouse and eye and, depending on period, the stay ran to a pair of deadeyes and lanyard, or a pair of closed hearts and lanyard on the aft face of the mainmast. Again, there were occasions when it ran to a block on the mainmast before being taken down to a lanyard and thimble on deck, **Mouse and Eye.** Shown in **Fig.18.12**. A length of thread selected for the stay is passed around the mizzen masthead and leaving sufficient length of free end to form an eye, the required position of the mouse is assessed. It is not practical at the scales normally encountered to raise a mouse in the proper manner, so an overhand knot to act as a stopper is usually adequate. The eye is then formed on the end of the stay. This would normally be an eye spliced into the end of the stay, but again for practical purposes, I fix the free end with a couple of seizings. The eye is then passed around the masthead from port to starboard and the other end of the stay passed through the eye and pulled up until it is stopped by the mouse. The procedure shown in **Fig.18.12**, uses natural thread for the purposes of clarity.

Closed Hearts . One of the closed hearts is fitted to the main mast the other to the lower end of the stay, leaving a gap between them that is partially pulled up by a lanyard. A fair degree of tension is required in the stay to avoid its alignment being distorted when later rigging, such as crowsfeet and braces, are added. Thus, the fixing of the closed heart to the mast needs to be strong and a multiple overhand knot should be considered. Blocks for the later rigging of the braces should be added.

Main Stay and Preventer

Starting from the main top with a mouse and eye and, with a closed heart in its lower end, the stay ran past the foremast on the starboard side, the lower heart being between the foremast and the forecastle rail, **Fig.18.1**.

Collar. This was essentially a strop attached to the prow of the ship and around the bowsprit and which passed through the forecastle rails where a heart was seized. Tension in the mainstay was taken up by means of a lanyard between the two hearts.

Preventer. Usually rigged to the main top just above the mainstay with a mouse and eye, it was rigged either to the rear face of the foremast, the bowsprit or the forecastle deck. In the case of the bowsprit fixing it passed the foremast on the starboard side but when fixed to the deck it passed to port. These lower fixings vary according to date.

Snaking. This was a line securing the stay proper to the preventer. It was rigged between them in zigzag fashion from the mouse to the lower heart, each point of the zigzag being seized alternately to the stay and the preventer, **Fig.18.14**.

I start at the mouse seizing the line at each point with an overhand knot, using a pair of dividers to keep the spacing of the zigzag constant. The snaking should be of fairly soft thread to maintain a degree of sharpness at the points of the zigzag. Dilute PVA is then brushed on and allowed to thoroughly dry before trimming the seizings close.

Blocks for the later rigging of braces should be added to the stays at this stage. See Chapter Nineteen.

Forestay and Preventer

These are rigged in a similar manner to the mainstay. With a mouse and eye at the foretop, the stay and preventer are rigged at their bottom ends to the bowsprit with closed hearts, or deadeyes and lanyards. The lower deadeye or heart was secured to the bowsprit by a collar.

Snaking. The stay and its preventer may, or may not, have been snaked together, depending on period or class of vessel. Any blocks required for rigging the spritsail braces etc. should be added at this stage. Topmast Stays and Preventers

These are rigged in a similar manner to other stays but are sometimes taken down to the deck by means of long tackle, (refer back to **Fig.17.1**).

Crowsfeet to the Tops

The crowsfeet prevent the bottom edge of the sail from chafing on the rim of the top. A euphroe block, having half the number of holes as the rim of the top, is rigged on the upper side of the stay in front of, and below, the top using a tackle with two single blocks, **Fig.18.15**.

Carefully measure and cut a sufficient length of natural thread to rig the crowsfeet, tie a stopper knot at one end and cyanoacrylate a bodkin at the other. The bodkin is passed *up* through the hole in the top immediately to the port side of centre until the stopper is against the underside of the top. It then passes down to the first hole in the euphroe block (the hole nearest the top) and back up to the top where it is threaded *down* through the hole next to centre on the starboard side. The bodkin is then fed *up* through the second hole on the starboard side and down to the second hole in the euphroe block before going back to the top and *down* through the second hole on the port side. This process continues until all holes around the front rim of the top have been rigged.

Don't try to attain final tension during the threading part of the operation, get the entire system rigged first. Start the tensioning at the centre of the rim and follow the crowsfeet in the same order as they were threaded. Try to keep the thread sharp cornered at the entrance and exit of the holes in the euphroe block but at the same time not distorting the line of the stay to which it is tied, again see **Fig.18.14**.

The main features of standing rigging are shown in **Figs.17.1** and **Fig.17.2** in the previous chapter.

CHAPTER NINETEEN

Running Rigging

It is somewhat outside the scope of this book to go into the detail of every part of the rigging that forms the working part of the sailing process. The drawings in today's kits do, for the most part, show the modeller where everything starts, what passage it takes and to where it is belayed. Rather than repeat such visual information in word form, this chapter endeavours to highlight areas where things can go wrong and how to avoid them. It may even refer to items that kit drawings fail to mention, although somewhat necessary to the finished appearance of the model. In summary, the drawings tell you what and where, but not always how and when.

The running rigging is put up using natural thread and, unless the thread provided in the kit is of particularly poor quality and very hairy, I do not normally give it the PVA finger treatment.

Tying Blocks

One of the fundamental techniques involved in putting up running rigging is tying blocks and this is something that can vary according to the scale of the model being constructed. What you don't want is a gigantic knot at the back of the block that is almost as big as the block itself! In fact, for most applications a simple running noose is adequate with the short end tidied up with or without a seizing according to size. If tackle is required on the other side of the block,

the line can be fitted in the same way. To avoid problems with accessibility, do this at the same time as fitting the block.

At smaller scales, I sometimes break my own rules, twist the thread around the block and

Fig. 19.1 Methods of block tying.

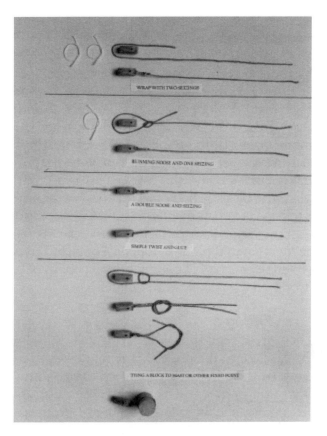

Fig. 19.2 Two-row parrels.   **Fig. 19.3 Jeers to lower yards.**

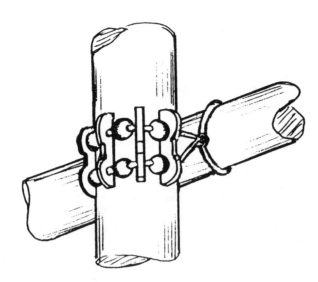

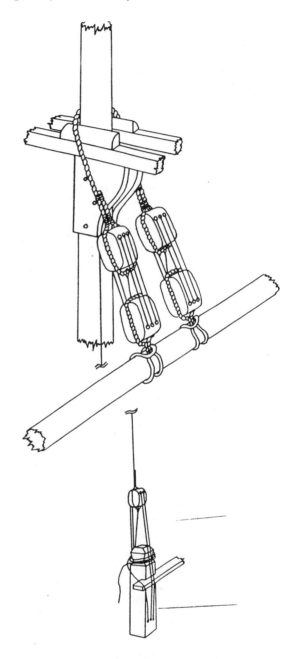

apply a small smear of cyanoacrylate. You have to be quick and positive, or you finish up with the whole thing stuck to your fingers, but with a little practice you can produce a neat job. Various ways of tying blocks for model making are shown in **Fig.19.1**.

That takes care of tying a block onto the end of a line, but what about a block that needs to be tied close to a mast or spar? I start the same way as before with a noose, but this time forming the noose in the centre of the length of thread so that when it is pulled up to the back of the block (the back being the end nearest the hole), the ends of the thread are about equal. Both strands of thread are then tied in an overhand knot and pulled up tight about 2mm behind the block. This is so that when the block is tied onto the mast or spar it is free to take up its natural position when reeved with the rigging with which it is associated. To tie the prepared block to the mast or spar, I use a multiple overhand knot, giving the whole block stropping a brushing with dilute PVA.

Fitting and Rigging the Yards

There are several approaches to actually putting the yards onto the masts. Some modellers prefer to fix them before stepping the masts, some like to do it after the masts have been put up and others, like myself, add them as I progress

with the significant parts of the running rigging. It is entirely a matter for personal choice and how convenient it is to your particular way of working.

Spritsail Yard.

This is the first yard I usually fit using a wire peg and truss. The remainder of the bowsprit rigging and the running rigging to the yard can now be completed with the exception of the braces, which

Fig. 19.4 Ties to upper yards.

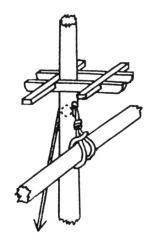

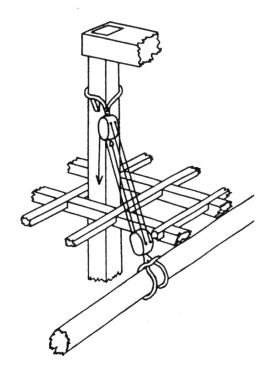

I leave until after all the yards on the foremast have been rigged.

Fore Yard.

I next work on the fore yard, using the brass peg in the back to hold it in position while I rig the parrels or trusses, **Fig.19.2**, then the jeers, **Fig.19.3**.

Parrels. The lower yards would probably have three rows of ribs and trucks, the upper yards

two, and the boom and gaff one row of trucks only across the mouth of the jaws at their butt end. A tidy way to make the parrels is to tie lengths of thread together leaving sufficient at the short end to tie to the yard. The longer lengths are then bodkined with cyanoacrylate and threaded into the first rib. Alternately, trucks and ribs are added until the parrels go right around the mast. The number of trucks and ribs has to be judged by trial and error. When the correct length of parrels has been achieved, the long ends can be knotted off close to the last rib. It should be noted that ribs are frequently shaped on their outer side thus requiring them all to be threaded the same way round!

Trusses. These superseded parrels in the latter half of the eighteenth century, two pendants being used for the lower yards rigged by block and tackle to the deck close to the bottom of the mast.

Ties, Lifts and Buntlines. Having got the yard secure on the foremast, I then add the lifts and, if called for, the buntlines since the blocks on the underside of the top are reasonably accessible. Ties are detailed in **Fig.19.4**.

Fore Topsail Yard and Topgallant Yard. These are pegged to the mast after which a similar procedure is adopted as used for the foreyard, i.e. parrels, tie, halyard and lift.

Clue-lines and Sheets to the Upper Yards

After the topgallant yard has been put in place and the initial rigging done as for the two lower yards on the foremast, I then work on the topsail yard clues and sheets, before doing the same on the topgallant yard. For reasons of accessibility, I leave the clues, sheets and tacks to the fore course until after all other rigging has been done.

The clue line is tied to the yard about a third of the way out from its centre, passes through the block on the end of the sheet, back up to a block on the yard, then down to its belaying point on deck. The sheet comes down from the clue-line, through a sheave in the outer end of the yard, then along the yard to a block and on down to its belaying point on deck.

The knack here is to achieve balance in the

Fig. 19.5 Running rigging.

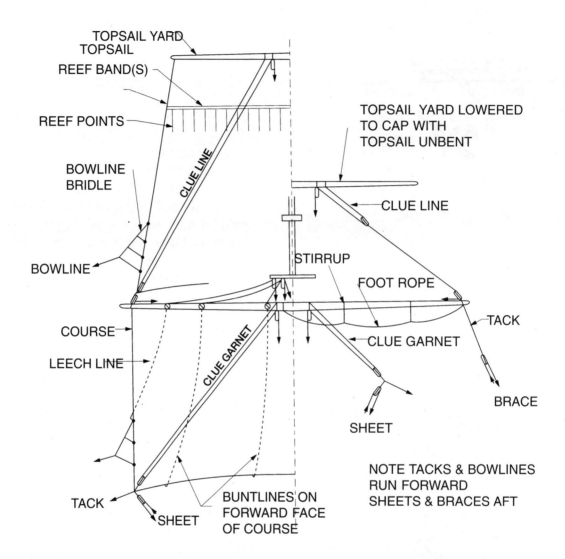

system so that port and starboard sheet blocks are hoisted to identical positions, not that they tried to do that on the ship, but because it looks pretty lopsided on your model if you don't!

The other thing to watch for is a straight passage of the clue-line and the sheet down to their respective belaying points. Take the line round the bottom of the belaying pin and gently pull it up taut then look to see if it fouls on any other rigging on its way down. Be prepared to do this a couple of times before making your final tie off.

The major items of running rigging are shown in **Fig.19.5**.

Yards on the Main Mast

These are fitted and rigged in the same manner as the yards on the foremast.

Yards on the Mizzen Mast. If the mizzenmast is rigged with a lateen yard it is generally better to put this on first, again using a wire peg and truss, followed by the tackle at its lower end. The remaining yards are then added in the same way as for the foremast and mainmast.

Backstays

I usually leave these features until about this stage of the rigging process because they do have a tendency to get in the way of hands and

Fig. 19.6 Fore yard tack and sheet.

fingers. They are rigged in a similar fashion to the shrouds, that is, via deadeyes and lanyards. The deadeyes are usually smaller in size and fitted to the aft end of the channels. Backstays to the uppermost masts may be mounted on stools fixed to the hull behind the channels.

Braces

If you have worked in accordance with many instruction manuals, you will have fitted the brace pendants when finishing off the yards and left them hanging. I choose to leave the rigging of the braces until nearly the end of the process, again for reasons of convenience and accessibility.

There is one significant difference with the rigging of braces to that of most other rigging and that is they should be left slack. Unfortunately, the thread provided in many kits seems to have a mind of its own and seldom wants to hang in the correct manner. Not only is it reluctant to adopt that nice catenary curve but insists on being wilful in the other plane as

well. There are one or two dodges that frequently prove successful but it is impossible to generalise due to variations in thread quality.

Cut off sufficient thread of the right diameters and wash in warm water with a touch of washing up liquid then hang it up to dry with weights on the bottom. The weight tends to stretch the thread and take out the natural twist. With the dressing washed out and less natural twist, the thread should be more amenable to coaxing into the catenary curve required. To assist further, once the brace is rigged and the required sag attained, the thread can be brushed with dilute PVA and the rigging stroked into a permanent shape with the underside of a piece of dowel or even a pencil.

It may be that the glue treatment and the stroking alone may be sufficient for some materials without having to pre-wash.

Alternatively, the braces can be rigged fairly taut. This is not truly correct, but many consider it better than a poor sagging brace due to the use of wilful thread.

Fig. 19.7 Hanks of rope in place on rails.

Clue-garnets, Tacks and Sheets to the Lower Yards

These are the last of the major lines to be rigged. The sheets, which would be attached to the bottom corner of the fore and main courses are rigged aft and pass through holes in the side of the hull to be belayed on cleats on the inside of the bulwarks. The tacks are rigged forward from the same corner of the sail. From the fore course they would go to a block on the end of the boomkin, then inboard to be belayed probably on the forecastle deck. From the main course the tack would run to the chess tree on the side of the hull, through the bulwarks to be tied off at a cleat.

However, if you don't have sails, the tack and the sheet are hoisted out of the way by the clue-garnets, which are rigged to the fore and main yards, (Fig.19.6). The tack, sheet and clue garnet blocks should be put together on the bench prior to rigging the overall system.

Rope Hanks and Coils

This is one area that is often neglected, both by the kit manufacturer and the kit builder. Where lines are belayed, what is left over after belaying is either coiled or hanked, hung on the relevant pin rail, or laid on the deck. The hanks and coils are made separately on the model and positioned after belaying, do not try to form them from the residue of the actual rigging.

How much rope is there in a coil or hank? Strictly speaking, the answer is, enough so that when the belaying is released, there is an adequate length for that part of the rigging to fulfil its function without the free end flying halfway up the mast where nobody can reach it! This may well be an important factor should the model be exhibited in competition. However, in general terms, five or six turns provide a coil that looks pretty good without being too bulky and awkward to handle.

Another thing to watch is that the coil is made from the same size and shade of thread as the rigging to which it is attached. I usually have a count and note how many in each size of thread I need then make them all in one go. I include hanks in the count since they are only coils requiring one additional operation.

To make a basic coil, I wind the thread around a slightly tapered dowel. In fact, the handle of an old paintbrush serves quite well, where you can select the point to wind the coil according to the diameter of coil needed. Five or six turns are normally enough before using a dab of cyanoacrylate to fix the ends in place. If you make sure that the finish of the winding is in the same place as the start, the adhesive works on both ends. With practice, the coil can be released from the tapered dowel before the adhesive really goes off it then only remains to trim the ends close.

To form a hank, there are two options. One is to take an untrimmed end of a basic coil and hitch it around the body of the turning. This is fine if your fingers are fairly dextrous, but if they are all like thumbs, pinch the coil together between thumb and forefinger and drop an open overhand knot over one end and pull it up. A further dab of cyanoacrylate and a close trim will finish the job.

Adding them to the model can be a little problematical due to accessibility and, while hanks should really be hung onto the relevant belaying pin, on smaller scale models this can be difficult. A major problem arises due to the stiffness of the thread which, having got the hank nicely hooked onto the pin, you find that it sticks out at an angle rather than hanging down naturally towards the deck. Trying to correct this with judiciously placed blobs of adhesive is hazardous to say the least and invariably finishes up looking a bit of a mess. One answer is not to hang them in the first place, but stick the hank to the front edge of the pin rail or rack, **Fig.19.7**.

Coils are glued flat onto the deck adjacent to the end of the tackle, with which they are associated, **Fig.12.5**. If you hang a coil anywhere, do not forget to alter its shape from circular to oval.

Flags

There are three points to remember with flags, make sure that you use the right ones, check that you fly them in the right place, and ensure that they look like proper flags. The first two items can be readily handled by doing a bit of research should you suspect that the kit instructions and drawings are questionable. Making them look like flags is more a case of practice.

The methods to be adopted vary according to the quality of the material onto which the flag has been printed. Silk is a favourite with many modellers because it has the potential to hang correctly. However, like all materials it has its own inherent problems which require to be attended to before trying to mount and shape. Frayed edges are definitely out and the edges of the flags as supplied ought to be sealed before trimming to final size. A thorough soaking in warm water will soften the material and, after drying, the edges can be sealed with PVA adhesive.

The edge that is nearest to the flagstaff is known as the hoist and, for model flags, this edge should have sufficient material to fold a seam over a length of rigging thread.

Doing the actual folding can be a bit fiddly and a touch of UHU adhesive may be of assistance to keep the rigging thread right back into the inside of the fold. If you are really careful, cyanoacrylate will also do the trick but it does need to be kept under control and not allowed to spread onto the face of the flag. It has one advantage in that it stiffens the hoist and provides a sound basis from which to form the "hang."

Getting the flag to hang right, as I have already said, is a matter of practice and involves two basic procedures, the rolled shape and the concertina shape, applied either vertically to the flag for the "stiff breeze" effect, or at varying angles for the "hanging limp" appearance. Fingers and thumbs are the best tools, but remember that when the flag is flown, the back edge is nominally straight.

CHAPTER TWENTY

Where Kits Come From

This chapter lists most of the major kit producers and a selection of their products. The choice of these particular kits is made purely and simply on the grounds that I have made them all and prepared in-depth reviews for each of them. The three volumes of The Period Ship Handbook include all those selected below as well as many others.

AMATI

This company has been in production for over 100 years and, in that time has built up a fine reputation for quality kits. Amati also produces a very comprehensive range of spares and accessories – very useful for kit enhancement.
H.M.S. Bounty comes from the Amati Collection of Museum Quality models. With a bit of further research a truly fine and historically accurate model of this most popular and fascinating ship can be made.
Scale 1:60, overall length 750mm.
H.M.S. Bounty was reviewed in Model Boats magazine in March 1999
Retail and trade distribution by Euro Models, 35 Crown Road, St.Margarets, Twickenham. TW1 3EJ

ARTESANIA LATINA

This Spanish company produces kits for a very wide range of ship models. There is something in their catalogue for all degrees of craftsman-

ship and newcomers to the hobby will certainly find a kit that will match their needs. The more experienced are not forgotten either and there are many kits to test their skills.
Le Hussard, a French navy schooner, is the subject of a kit from the middle of the Artesania range in terms of difficulty. It is an unusual vessel having a rotating carronade at bow and stern.
Scale 1:50, overall length 735mm.
La Toulonnaise, is a very attractive French Goelette for modellers with average skills.
Scale 1:70, overall length 720mm.
Le Hussard and *La Toulonnaise* were reviewed in Model Boats magazine in April 1995 and May 1991 respectively.
Trade only distribution by Toyway, P.O.Box 55, Unit 20, Jubilee Trade Centre, Letchworth, Herts. SG6 1SG

BILLING

A Danish company providing graded kits for beginner and experienced model makers. They have developed their own construction system based on building the hull in two halves. Fittings are usually a mixture of wooden, brass and plastic parts.
The FD10 Yawl is a subject ideally suited to the less experienced and makes up into a very attractive model.
Overall length 700mm.
Will Everard is typical of many of the vessels

that plied the East coast of England that had a charisma all of their own.

Overall length 580mm.

Both kits were reviewed in Model Boats magazine in May 1989

Trade only distribution by Amerang Ltd. Commerce Way, Lancing, West Sussex. BN15 8TE

COREL

Another old and well-established company that has been producing high quality kits since 1971. Timber quality, together with castings and photo-etched parts can be anticipated to be of the highest order.

One of Corel's more recent additions to their range is the kit for *H.M.S. Bellona*. Not a beginners' package, this "74" nevertheless makes up into a fine exhibition model after many hours of meticulous work. Scale 1:100. Overall length 770mm.

H.M.S. Bellona was reviewed in Model Boats magazine in May 2000

The *Leida* is one of Corel's latest offerings for the beginner and must be rated at one of the best there is in that class. There is nothing too difficult in construction or rigging to put anyone off, but enough of a challenge to keep the interest going.

Scale 1:64. Overall length 350mm.

Leida was reviewed in Model Boats magazine in February 2002

Retail and trade distribution by Euro Models, 35 Crown Road, St.Margarets, Twickenham. TW1 3EJ

CALDERCRAFT

Superb kits designed by people who know what kit builders want. Excellent instruction manuals and drawings supported by in-depth research. Good quality materials, a mass of accurately produced pre-cut parts are complemented by castings and fittings dedicated to the particular vessel in hand. These are top-flight products from a British company with a rapidly expanding range.

The kit for *H.M.S. Cruiser* is one in the *Nelson's Navy* series that sets a new standard for a kit builder-friendly package. The accuracy of fit on all pre-cut parts is superb and all castings and other fittings are specific to the vessel in hand. This, and other kits in the Nelson's Navy series, brings competition and museum standard model making to many more modellers.

Scale 1:64. Overall length 850mm.

H.M.S. Cruiser was reviewed in Model Boats magazine in July 2000

H.M.S. Agamemnon is one of the larger kits in the Nelson's Navy series. It measures 1.3 metres long and features all the expertise that can be brought to bear in modern kit production. A model of a 64-gun ship of the line that has everything for the experienced model maker.

Scale 1:64. Overall length 1300mm.

H.M.S. Agamemnon was reviewed in Model Boats magazine in August and September 2002

H.M.S. Victory is, in every sense, the flagship of the Nelson's Navy range of kits. It lays claim to being the most accurate reproduction of this famous vessel as it was at Trafalgar in 1805, all research being verified by the Keeper and Curator of *H.M.S. Victory* at Portsmouth. The kit content is superb in every way and provides many hundreds of hours pure enjoyment for the experienced kit builder.

Scale 1:72. Overall length 1385mm with a height of 940mm and a beam of 525mm.

H.M.S. Victory will be reviewed in Model Boats magazine early in 2004

Retail and trade distribution by JoTiKa Ltd. Marine Warehouse, Hadzor, Droitwich, Worcs.

EUROMODEL COMO

Kits from this company are of high quality but are really for the more experienced model maker. The drawings are superb in their detail but instructions for building are virtually non-existent. Good quality materials and fittings throughout.

The Renommee is a French 42-gun frigate from 1793 and the kit is quite a challenge for any model maker. Be prepared for over a thousand hours of work to produce a first class model.

Overall length 838mm.

Reviewed in Model Boats magazine in September, October and November 1993

Retail and trade distribution by Euro Models,

35 Crown Road, St.Margarets, Twickenham, TW1 3EJ

MAMOLI

This company, founded many years ago by Luigi Volante, has earned a good reputation in the market place and provides a wide range of interesting subjects from which to choose.

The brigantine *Portsmouth* is a nice one for the relative beginner and has enough demanding constructional features to maintain interest. The drawings and rigging details are particularly good for the less experienced.

Britannia, the racing yacht built for Edward VII, is a beautifully lined craft and while the kit is not for the absolute beginner, it does provide an interesting and pleasant change from the sailing man of war.

Scale 1:64. Overall length 760mm with a height of 960mm.

Reviewed in Model Boats magazine in July 1994

Trade distribution by Amerang Ltd. Commerce Way, Lancing, West Sussex, BN15 8TE

THE MANTUA GROUP - PANART

This Italian group is in the top echelon of kit manufacturers and can be relied upon to provide good quality materials and fittings. It produces kits for a very wide range of subjects each one being excellent value for money.

The Panart kit for the *Royal Caroline* must be one of the most popular kits around and cer-tainly provides excellent value for money. In the middle of the range as far as complexity is concerned, it provides an ornate addition to any collection.

Scale 1:47 Overall length 815mm.

Reviewed in Model Boats magazine in September 1994

Also from Panart comes the kit for the *1803 Armed Pinnace*. This package provides a departure, not only from the usual range of subjects offered in kit form, but also in terms of the construction techniques involved. The scale lends itself to excellent detail work and the results are a model of great charm and of a size that permits effective display in most domestic environments.

Scale approx. 1:16 Overall length 620mm.

Reviewed in Model Boats magazine in December 1993

Retail and trade distribution by Euro Models, 35 Crown Road, St.Margarets, Twickenham, TW1 3EJ

VICTORY MODELS LTD

A new company on the British scene formed in association with Euro Models of Twickenham and Amati of Turin. A series of kits starting with one for the beginner, *The Lady Nelson,* and all featuring the design expertise of international model maker, Chris Watton, promise to be a welcome addition to the quality end of the market place.

INDEX